SMARTER STARTING

BUILDING A TINY BUSINESS

Sierra Bailey

Smarter Starting: Building a Tiny Business

For more information, contact:
Sierra Bailey
sierra@mssierrabailey.com
www.mssierrabailey.com

Library of Congress Control Number: 2021913159

ISBN 978-1-7374788-1-2 (paperback)

Printed in the United States

Edited by Mallory Lehenbauer | Mallory Katherine
Book cover by Joanna Holden | Modular, ink.

First edition published July 2021

Dedicated to Joann Bailey aka Ga,

Who, from the beginning modeled for me what it means to be a Doer Shaker Maker.

Contents

PART I:

The Foundation of Your Tiny Business

Introduction:

How Tiny Businesses Are Born

At dinner a few years ago, I was sitting next to a fellow talented, tiny business owner and we were talking the way we do, swapping stories and offering advice to each other. A friend of a friend sat down and said that she wished she owned a business…so that she could work fewer hours and do whatever she wanted all day long as we did. This was followed by silence and blank stares from both of us.

At the time, I was still running a jewelry brand and the friend was a personal trainer. We were both exhausted, although I don't remember it being a busy season for either of us, simply a Tuesday night.

Sure, she was fresh out of college and worked in a law firm, so she had a skewed perspective of the hours someone employed by someone else would work, but still, we could only tilt our heads in wonder at her comment and finally laugh in response. She had no idea what the reality of owning a business was really like. She most likely didn't grow up with parents or family members who were entrepreneurs, and her views were formed from reading success stories and watching Shark Tank. That or she was picking a fight.

Either way, let's clear this up. We all think we know what it will be like before we start. But it's so different when you are in the middle of it. When you are living through days that begin at 6 a.m. and finish (and how many business owners ever feel finished?) at 6 p.m. on a regular basis. Not everyone chooses to work these hours, but for many of us, it's the love of the work itself that brought us to self-employment. That near-obsession with wanting to show up and do this thing every day is what has driven most tiny business owners to take the leap.

You're not pushed by the thought of quick riches or dreams of working only one hour a day. Rather, you're driven by a love of what you do. You want to run your own show. You don't want to manage a big team or staff. You want to be able to do the work you love and do it in your own little bubble. You hope that once you have established a strong foundation for your business, you will be able to step back if you choose. However, if you want to achieve a six or seven-figure income or have a business that will last more than a few years? You will need to put in the time and hard work to create that solid foundation that you can build on top of.

If you picked up this book and are excited about breaking a

million in sales year one or can't wait to kick back and enjoy the easy life, you're probably going to be disappointed. But if you are reading this with a twinkle in your eye, a head full of ideas, and you cannot wait to get started—know that this was written for you.

What Is All This Talk About Tiny Businesses?

A few years ago, I started calling businesses with five or fewer employees, tiny. Why? Well, according to the SBA (Small Business Association), a small business is any business with 500 or fewer employees.[1] That struck me as odd, as those are such different businesses than the ones I see every day. It makes you wonder how they can even be in the same category. Interestingly, small businesses in the US are shrinking in employee size but growing in revenue. That's a really good sign! In fact, 99.9% of all businesses in the US are considered small businesses.[2] And yes. I agree that this all seems ridiculous. Why not make a few categories to help differentiate? Because really, all businesses except for the 0.1%, which you can name them easily, the Uber's, the Google's, the H&R Blocks, and are classified as Enterprises, are considered small businesses. How is this a thing?

---

1 The SBA determines business size for the ability to obtain government contracts: https://www.sba.gov/sites/default/files/advocacy/2018-Small-Business-Profiles-US.pdf

2 SBE Council and Facts & Data on Small Business and Entrepreneurship: https://sbecouncil.org/about-us/facts-and-data/

I'll give the SBA a bit of credit, there is one more level of small businesses. The classification for very small businesses means less than 50 employees.

What does this mean? That almost all businesses are considered small businesses. And many are so much bigger than what most of us ever want to own. If you are looking at a course or a service marketed towards small businesses, the chances are high that it will not be geared towards tiny businesses. It may be priced for a 400-person business or created to benefit a business with 80 employees. In short, you are faced with information (for example about the management of large teams), systems (for sales teams, not people), and costs (services that cost more than your business may make in a year). These topics are not even in the same universe of what you are probably looking for.

Another fact is that two-thirds of businesses make it to two years, half make it five years, and one-third of businesses make it 10 years. It is very tough to have a business going for a decade. A depressing statistic is that 86.3% of small business owners take a salary of less than a hundred thousand dollars and 30% of small business owners take zero salaries.[3] The average CEO makes $160,000 a year, the *average* CEO[4]. If you are the CEO of your own small business and taking zero salaries, you're working for

3 Fundera has some sad facts about small business owners salaries: https://www.fundera.com/blog/study-finds-business-owners-earn-less

4 For a look at what CEOs who are not Fortune 500 level make: https://www.payscale.com/research/US/Job=Chief_Executive_Officer_(CEO)/Salary

free for something that may not make it more than two years.

If a small business has outside financing (money from beyond the sales within the business), 75% of that financing is coming from either business loans, business credit cards, or lines of credit. The other 25% is from personal savings, friends and family investment, or Kickstarter, or something similar. They are rarely VC funded or have had large amounts of cash handed to them just to see what they can do. Tiny businesses, especially in the first few years, are often excluded from traditional funding sources, as banks require two years of P&L (Profit & Loss) statements and most tiny businesses are not aiming to sell quickly or go public.

The reality is that 29% of businesses fail from a lack of cash flow. While 42% fail for lack of market need[5]. And unfortunately, for the talented people that create businesses around their talent, well, the market doesn't always want what people are talented in.

So where do Tiny Businesses fit into the definition of small businesses? Well, the SBA has added a classification for these. Businesses with 1-9 employees are technically called Micro Businesses[6]. And there are a ton of them. The term micro however just doesn't sound as good with business as tiny does though. So

---

5 To see the stats from the US Bureau of Labor Statistic via Fundera: https://www.fundera.com/blog/what-percentage-of-small-businesses-fail

6 More charts about Micro Businesses: https://advocacy.sba.gov/2017/08/01/the-role-of-microbusiness-employers-in-the-economy/

I have taken it upon myself to rename these businesses and focus on the smallest of them, those with 5 or fewer employees. About 75% of small businesses in the U.S. are Micro businesses and about 45% of small businesses are single owners and operators. That means you're in great company! It's okay to set out to build a tiny business. Especially for those who love freedom and flexibility (more on that in a minute). Don't feel like you have to have 30 employees or make $2 million a year in order to be successful. Create your own idea of what success looks like, take action and you'll be amazed at what you can do.

Just keep in mind that being in business for yourself is going to be vastly different, well, everything, than being a business with 500 employees. Unfortunately, this means that so much information out there for small businesses feels completely irrelevant to you. Because it is. It's written for the 50-500 employee small business owners. Which frustrated me to the point that I realized that I wanted to create a change. Everything you are about to read in this book is written for tiny businesses. Why?

Because I am a huge fan of tiny businesses and have had a fantastic unconventional career thanks to owning and running my own since 2002. With my last business, I soared past the 10-year mark and profited for the entire 16 years. I closed that business because I craved new challenges and felt such a drive to help people, just like you, learn how to start and run amazing tiny businesses. And then I immediately started my current Tiny Business.

I want you to love owning a tiny business as much as I do, but like that friend of a friend at the beginning of the chapter, I don't want you to jump in blindly. You need to know what you're signing up for. But you also should get excited and I can't wait to see you soar!!

Chapter 1:

The Good, The Bad & The Euphoric

The Good

Let's begin with the amazing parts of owning a tiny business. There are so many wonderful aspects of owning a business that far outweighs the bad for most of us, so before I freak you out, let's talk about the sunshine and rainbows.

Number One - Freedom

The reality is that tiny businesses have the most freedom of them all. In owning a tiny business, you have the potential to develop revenue streams where you can be earning money beyond trading your hours for dollars. Tiny businesses, unlike the larger small businesses, tend to not have many employees, if any. This gives you a huge amount of flexibility as you will have no one to answer to or to be responsible for besides your clients.

This is why so many stay-at-home parents opt to start tiny businesses. Because you can create the most flexibility with your schedule and still have the potential for a high income. You can also have a super weird schedule if you prefer. If you have kids and need to be home at a specific time, it's no problem. If you love to go to Tuesday matinees, it can be done. If you want to take off two months a year to travel, you can build this into your business.

Simply put, with a tiny business, you can determine the parameters. As long as your customers and clients are communicated with and are aware that you'll be gone, you can hit the road carefree.

Number Two - Ability to Pivot Quickly

When you run a tiny business, you can accomplish things much faster. You make all decisions how you see fit. This has less to do with control and more about making quick decisions and getting things done. It starts with the branding, the marketing, and the problems you are solving. These are all up to you. If you decide that you want to introduce a new product, you can get that product out as fast as you can get your hands on it, via wholesale or by creating it. You don't even have to have your hands on it if you are dropshipping.

If your current products or services are not selling, you can change directions quickly. There are many factors that make it easier to make quick changes, one being that it's simply less stressful to change than if you had a bigger business or more employees. The ability to move quickly and cheaply never became more of an advantage than when the Covid pandemic settled in. The tiny businesses were for the most part able to adapt the fastest. Partially due to their size and partially for the third good item on our list.

Number Three - Low Overhead

If you are a tiny business, your overhead will be lower than larger small businesses. Most tiny businesses are based out of their homes. Not having to pay for office space or a brick-and-mortar space can be huge in keeping overhead low. If it's just you, you don't have to have pens and computers and tech support for your staff. This means your office equipment overhead will be lower. If it's just you or you have contract workers, not employees, you are not paying to process payroll or for health insurance and benefits. It is less expensive to pay for health insurance for just you than it is to pay for employees. This can make owning a tiny business less risky as you're not necessarily putting in as much capital, you're not taking loans from investors and you are not putting as much upfront yourself.

Number Four - Working Solo

You get to work alone. This comes up repeatedly, almost apologetically with tiny business owners. Many of us love community and collaboration, but we love to work on our own even more. Again, it's a draw for introverts and the flip side of the negative we just went over. I myself am a very loud, secret introvert. When I'm around people, I never shut up, and then I immediately need a nap. I enjoy one-on-one meetings and small groups, but big groups overwhelm me. The idea of working in a big company makes me want to lie down and sleep forever. I bet many of you are nodding your heads as you read this, if you're not, understand that there are many of us who feel this way. Also, the no boss thing. That's a big deal for many of us. A big positive, awesome, big deal.

Number Five - Limitless Growth Potential

There are no limits. You can grow as big as you want to. Where you go and how you grow is up to you. Even with a tiny business of 5 employees or less, you can have a booming business with annual sales in the millions. The amount of work, the number of clients, the amount you sell, is only limited by you. You get to determine what you will achieve.

Number Six - You Call the Shots

You can stop whenever you want. This is a big one which you don't realize how important it is until after it happens. I owned a business for almost 16 years and by the end, I felt trapped by it. I felt that it was wrong of me to not love the business anymore and do not want the dream job I created for myself. We tell ourselves a lot of stories until they're true. The only truth is that you can stop at any time and it's not the wrong thing to do. In fact, sometimes admitting that you no longer want to be in that business is the rightest thing in the world.

The Bad

Now for a quick reality check. What does it really feel like to own a business? There may be people out there who never feel the things below, but I have yet to meet them. These are the big things that seem to dominate most of the bad columns for tiny business owners.

Number One - You'll Have No Idea What You're Doing

The first is a big one. You will constantly have no idea what you're doing. This can be terrifying for some people and great for others. The truth is, there is no playbook. Anyone who says you simply need to follow their formula to have wild success at what you are doing wants to sell you their formula. It's incredibly difficult to recreate and replicate success within your own business, forget about trying to recreate what someone else has done to achieve success in theirs.

You will need to constantly be learning and trying new things if you want to have a long-lasting and sustainable business that also fulfills you. Even if you know exactly what you're doing today, chances are that in the next day, week or month, you'll once again, have no idea how to do something.

Number Two - You Will Worry About Money

I had a childhood friend who started to work in his family business in the summers of high school. Immediately upon graduating from college, he was made a principal owner. It was a high-end pool business and although he had been working in the field for years, first helping build the pools and then managing the crews, he was not that familiar with the business side of it. He, like many of us who start a business around a skill or talent, had become excellent at making sure the pools were built outstandingly, that the customers were happy and that the crew was working to get all of this done. These are of course all important skills to have when running a business, but he had never had to balance the books, find new customers, work with vendors, or make any of the marketing decisions. One day I asked him what it was like to step into that side of it. He looked at me and said, "I now worry about money all the time. Constantly. From when I wake up to when I go to bed. It's always on my mind, there is no break from the worry." And this was someone who was taking over a family business that was incredibly successful and profitable. It turns out that he hated running the business side of it. He ended up stepping away from it a few years later.

You will worry about money. Even if you are getting, well, especially if you are getting outside funding, you will worry about money. If you need to get funding, you are worried about securing it. Once you have been funded, you worry about how you can make it last, make it grow, and make sure your investors are happy. If you are self-funded (and most tiny business owners are) you either put your savings on the line, borrowed from your friends and family or are racking up high-interest credit card debt (not ideal but this does happen often).

This can feel like a different pressure than you expect if you have never been responsible for all money coming in and going out. The reality is that it may take at least a year for a steady income to start coming in. It may take two years before you can start tracking your numbers and predicting your income. Few businesses take off immediately, and to keep growing you will have to put some money into it. You can bootstrap a good deal and as you'll come to learn, staying scrappy is a strong plan. But even if all you need is a website, a phone, and your time, there will still be taxes, fees, and overhead to pay for. It takes a lot of work to go from nothing to producing an income that covers both business expenses as well as pays you a salary for your living expenses.

You also may encounter supply chain struggles, because being a tiny business means you are not able to order large quantities from manufacturers. If you even are ordering enough to order straight from a manufacturer, you may be locked out of a lot of lower-cost options because you're just not working in the volume required. This may mean that you have to charge more compared to larger competitors. This is not necessarily a bad thing, but something to be aware of.

Number Three - Talent Is Expensive

The third can apply to most people who work, not just to business owners. But it does apply especially to tiny business owners as we juggle so many roles. Even those of us who are masters of productivity feel that at the end of the day, there is still so much more to be done. You may check off every item on that to-do list and feel like you have conquered the world, and then 5 minutes later, you are wondering "what would happen if you tried this one other thing?", or "what if you quickly created a piece of content to share?", or "you should really try out a new product". The to-do list feels like it never ends. Just as there is always more to learn, there is also, always more to do. Granted, there's a good chance that it's this personality trait that will make you a successful business owner, so this is only a bad thing if you let it be.

Number Four - It Can Feel Isolating

This one can be a big one if you are not used to working alone. Starting a business can feel isolating for the obvious reason, like that you no longer have people around you while working. If you are used to water cooler banter, grabbing lunch with your buddy a few doors down or chatting in the hall, you may feel this acutely. Except for the introverts, who really do want this isolation, this can be mentally tough to deal with. I'm starting to think that the allure of ample alone time is the reason why so many introverts start their own businesses.

However, even for introverts, the life of a tiny business owner can make you feel incredibly alone. There are endless decisions to be made and you are making them all on your own. Stressed about a client or money? All on you. The countless choices that feel huge and you have to make each day? All on you.

This isolation often comes from feeling like you in this all alone more than it comes from the lack of physical proximity to others. And in addition to the isolation, knowing that if it fails, it's all on you, can be a daunting fear for many.

Number Five - What You Love Is 20%

There's a good chance that you are starting a business around a skill you have cultivated over time. Perhaps you have been getting paid by a company to perform this skill for years. Maybe you have been cultivating a hobby and you're ready to make it a job. Or you have been studying and being trained in something and you're ready to jump in and start. In all these instances, you most likely have been focused on getting really good at this one specific thing. You know that thing inside and out.

This is excellent, as being great at your thing is important, but to have a successful business, you will end up doing that thing about 20% of the time. The rest of your time will be focused on marketing, sales, and ensuring that you are making money. If you are not selling your products or services, or are not creating a profit past year two for multiple years in a row, you have a hobby, not a business.

You will need to do more than just the thing you are good at to run a business successfully.

Starting a business can be incredibly eye-opening with the sheer volume of boring, mundane tasks that need to be regularly performed. It seems many people assume that when they start a business, they can outsource everything immediately. That's a nice idea in theory but remember that you have to pay to outsource work. Cheap labor does not yield the best results, so you will need to pay a lot of money to outsource to someone who does that work well. Even if you are using an automated tech option or third-world labor, you will still need to pay something in exchange for the work.

If you can afford to hire help, and even if you could pay for the top tier of talent, you are not going to attract the best to workers as you have little to offer compared to larger companies. It can be hard to attract talent if that talent has nowhere to grow. Or if you don't have much to offer that talent competitively salary and benefits wise.

You may not have six figures to pay a talented person to join your team. This means that you cannot compete against a lot of the corporations or the larger small businesses and therefore you simply won't get the talent. You for sure don't have stock options, and most likely are not offering equity (unless your plan is to not be tiny and grow to sell or go public). You are limited in what you can use to attract talent to work for you full time.

If you are looking at hiring contract work at an hourly rate, you are often priced out of hiring talented people. This is a big downside of wanting to bring on help as a tiny business, especially in the first two years.

When it comes to paying for business services, many of the service providers for small businesses create rates and packages to serve small businesses with 20 or more employees. They charge more than tiny business owners can or are willing to pay. There are, of course, incredible people who do prefer to work with tiny businesses, but you have to look for them and make sure you are getting solid referrals.

When you are able to pay to outsource, you have to meticulously know what you want them to do, or things will never work in your favor. This means that you need to put in the time to do the most boring and mundane tasks yourself first This will ensure that you can explain to someone and train them on how it needs to be done. Not doing this will be a waste of time for everyone and can quickly put you out of business. There is no quick and affordable solution to outsourcing.

Number Six - There Is No Playbook

There is no playbook. No two businesses are identical, so even if you do exactly what someone else has done, it may not yield the same results. The odd part is that even with that never-ending to-do list you have no idea most of the time if you are doing the right thing. It can be incredibly overwhelming to not have a path to walk on when you are in the middle of the forest.

Number Seven - You May Lack A Support System

One last thing that can creep up on you is your support system. In the beginning, everyone in your life will cheer you on and be your biggest supporters. But as time goes on, they are distracted by their own shiny objects or just are not as enthusiastic as they once were. This is not their fault, it's human nature. Spouses, partners and loved ones are supportive if they think that you will be happy and there will be income coming in to ensure security. When both of those are lacking for long periods of time, they sometimes are not as excited for you as they were in the beginning. They may not understand your drive and the need you have to keep going. They may even start to pressure you to quit. I always joke that all our spouses really want is for us not to cry and to make money. This may be a not so funny reality.

I'll touch on this more in a moment, but this is a good reason to not quickly jump to full-time in your business.

It Will Be Difficult. So What?

Alright, you get the idea. Owning a business is both amazing and scary. It takes a good deal of work, specific skills, and a certain mindset. You most likely will not make enough money to fully support yourself and the business for a year, maybe two. I'm not trying to stop you from starting, but rather preparing you for the reality of owning a business.

Most successful business owners are optimistic and take calculated risks. In owning a business, this breaks down to being able to do new things, yet first researching and weighing the options of what success and failure would look like. Getting excited about new things, but not jumping in blindly and understanding that one good windfall will not create an end all be all success story. That a successful business is made up of a series of decisions, and that you need to learn from both failures and successes. It's about continuously testing, trial and error and above all else, not being afraid of taking those calculated risks.

It can be incredibly stressful if you have never had to sell your work, to suddenly have to depend more on your ability to market and sell than any other skills. Most likely, at least for the first few months or years, it will continue to be all on you to do all of that work. At the start, you cannot hire out the sales, marketing, and admin work and only do the tasks you enjoy doing. That is actually exactly what it means to work for someone else. If that's what you want, then I'm glad you've realized it. Save the effort, time, and money, and go do that. There is no shame in being an employee. My husband loves corporate life. He loves knowing what the top is, reaching for it every day, and having a huge team around him to work with. Owning a small business has zero appeal to him. Working for someone else is the perfect place for him to shine and it may be for you too.

You should enjoy learning about the other parts of owning a business. As your work will most likely be 20% of what you like to do and 80% of what you have to do, it would be unfortunate to spend 80% of your time doing what you don't want to do. You should be excited about all of this!

For people who love to be constantly challenged, to help people, and to solve problems with their work, there is no greater feeling than when things go well in a business you own. Just be aware of the work and commitment it takes going into it. Of the emotional toll it can have, and most importantly that it's rarely about making money quickly.

Gary Vaynerchuk often shares that he would rather work 80 hours a week for himself than 40 hours for someone else. That sums up what drives many of us to start our own businesses. It's that desire to run our own show. If all of this sounds incredible and you are aware of the bad aspects, then buckle up and jump on it, it may be a bumpy ride, but it will be the ride of your life!

To Sum Up:

- The good parts of owning a business are flexibility, the ability to change quickly and nimbly, having alone time to focus, no limit on your potential, and having the ability to stop when you want.
- The bad parts of owning a business are that you will feel overwhelmed, be worried about money, wear all the hats in the beginning (even if they don't fit), feel isolated, not get to do the part you love that much, you won't know what you're doing much of the time, and that you may not feel supported.
- Yes, there are many bad parts. Yes, it will be a ton of work. But, the feeling of creating a business out of nothing and succeeding at it can be the best feeling in the world. Trust me.

Chapter 2:

Defining Your Own Success

What Does Success Look Like To You?

For one person, success may look like making a high income, or being debt free. For another person, it may be having a schedule that can allow for after school pickups and evenings and weekends off. For others it can be doing work you love and being able to turn away clients who don't align with your values.

There are two reasons why it's so important to ask yourself this question. First, because it will help you know what you are aiming for and second so that you'll know it when you get there. As a business owner, it will be thrilling when you achieve a goal you have been working so hard towards and then 10 minutes later, you'll ask yourself, now what?

This is probably unavoidable, and why celebrating all wins, big and small is essential. While those goals are whizzing by, you want to at least be aware that you are doing what you set out to do. That the thing you are doing is in fact, achieving success.

When you own a business, there is no one to give you a promotion, to tell you that you did a great job, or to take you out for a celebratory dinner. You'll need to do all of this yourself. By creating a bit of a road map for when to push and when to pat yourself on the back, you will create more fulfillment with your business.

If you ask most business owners what success looks like to them, you are going to hear one word over and over: freedom. I'm not sure they understand from what exactly, and I touched on this in the pros and cons list in chapter one, but *they* really like to say that. It's a big non-metric goal for people, and I think it's primarily stated by those who have worked in past careers where they had no control over their schedules. The freedom from being told when and where to do something is most likely behind that answer. Being able to sleep in if you're tired, pick the kids up from school every day, go to the 2 p.m. yoga class, and take a vacation whenever you want. If that's you, great, you'll want to define what that freedom means but, you're getting there. Some of us though, have had less strict careers, or maybe had a business in the past and think of having freedom in your schedule as normal and not something to strive for.

You may be starting to see that defining success is not that simple of an answer. Let's go over a few examples which may help you get your own thoughts on this in order.

We'll start with financial measures of success:

- Having a specific amount of money set aside for retirement and in savings.
- Having a specific income each year and month.
- Owning your home outright.
- Being debt-free.
- Reaching a level where your spouse can quit their job and work with you.
- Leaving a legacy for your children.

Quality of life measures of success:

- Being able to determine the hours you work.
- Having flex time.
- Getting to travel more or never having to travel again for work.
- Being able to work from anywhere.
- Having time to pursue your hobbies and interests.

Work measures of success:

- Deciding which clients you will work with.
- Selling products or services that you believe in.
- Doing work that aligns with your personal values and

mission.

- Giving back to the community.
- Employing people from your community and providing a fair living wage.

Specific measures that are a bit ego-based, but still ok to have.

- Being profiled in a media or news outlet you admire.
- Receiving a specific award in your industry.
- Having a book you've written available in bookstores.
- Having your work featured in a place, such as hanging in a gallery, being published in a journal, speaking at a conference, etc.

There are, of course, endless options for how you can measure success. The idea is that you need to have success defined specifically. Sure, you'll keep adding a new layer on top of it, but you need to know what you're aiming for.

Knowing what success means to *you* will help you with shiny object syndrome, keep you on track, and hopefully prevent you from chasing what every Instagram account seems to be doing with their business. When combined with knowing your values, your mission statement and your vision, it will provide a true north for you to measure how you're doing with your business and if you're on track with where you want to be. The best example of a goals list is from Jack Canfield.[7] He shares it publicly on his blog and updates it in real-time. It is now 130 items long. 109 of which he wrote down in 1989 when he was 45. In 2006, 21-lifetime goals were added to the list. He is now 70 and it's incredible that he shares this with the world!

Knowing what success means to *you* will help you with shiny object syndrome, keep you on track, and hopefully prevent you from chasing what every Instagram account seems to be doing with their business. When combined with knowing your values, your mission statement and your vision, it will provide a true north for you to measure how you're doing with your business and if you're on track with where you want to be.

Why Do It?

Like declaring your vision or mission, your why is coming from deeper than wanting to make money and put your creations out there. You can absolutely start a business without thinking or defining your why, vision or mission. There has been so much research done about how having a grasp of the psychology behind your drive will lead to getting through the lows in business that it's worth being open to.

As much as it's important to understand what success looks

7 You can see the list Jack Canfield keeps at http://www.thesuccessprinciples.com/jack-canfields-101-goals-list/

like, understanding your why or your purpose will be what keeps you pushing when work gets exhausting and tough. It will become the driving force behind what you are doing. It's often the thing that made you want to start a business in the first place. It may be what made you pick up this book and what has made you take starting a business seriously.

Understanding your why will provide beyond the drive through, it will make you happier and provide you with a more fulfilled life. Many authors write extensively about your Why. It's a big and fascinating subject and that if you're curious, I encourage you to look into it. For now, and for the purposes of this conversation, we are going to be a bit briefer.

Purpose/Your Why: Why you want to have a business beyond the financial gain aspect. This is your "I believe…" statement. Companies rarely share this publicly on their websites. It can be for you and you alone to know. It's what will drive you.

Vision: The impact you will have on your client's/customers lives and the world. It's where you want to go with your business. You should be excited to tell people this and make it publicly available.

Mission: An ambitious and achievable way that you will accomplish your purpose. It's all about today and what you are currently doing. You will also share this publicly.

That all sounds incredibly vague. Let's go through a few examples to understand the concepts better.

When I had my jewelry company, my mission was to create jewelry for women who wanted to have high quality, unique and colorful jewelry to make them feel like it represented their personalities. My vision was to create a jewelry brand for women to wear to work.

In my current business, my vision is to provide business owners with the tools and support they need to feel confident in running businesses that allow them to do the work they enjoy. My mission is to provide accessible support, education, and encouragement to business owners with 5 employees and under. My why is to use my unique skill set to help my community thrive.

Now we'll look at companies with household names so you can start to think about these businesses and how their mission, vision, and purpose align with what you see.

Mary Kay

- Purpose: To give unlimited opportunity to women.
- Vision: To provide women with an unparalleled opportunity for financial independence, career and personal fulfillment. To achieve total customer satisfaction by delivering the products and services that

enhance a woman's self-image and confidence. The principles we live by: Integrity and the Golden Rule must guide every business decision.

- Mission: To enrich women's lives, with 'an unparalleled business opportunity'.

Patagonia

- Vision: A love of wild and beautiful places demands participation in the fight to save them, and to help reverse the steep decline in the overall environmental health of our planet.
- Mission: Build the best product, cause no unnecessary harm, use business to inspire and implement solutions to the environmental crisis.

Disney

- Vision: Disney Company's corporate vision is to be one of the world's leading producers and providers of entertainment and information.
- Mission: The mission of The Walt Disney Company is to be one of the world's leading producers and providers of entertainment and information. Using our portfolio of brands to differentiate our content, services and consumer products, we seek to develop the most creative,

innovative and profitable entertainment experiences and related products in the world.

Airbnb

- Vision: Tapping into the universal human yearning to belong—the desire to feel welcomed, respected, and appreciated for who you are, no matter where you might be.
- Mission: Belong anywhere.

Southwest Airlines

- Vision: To become the world's most loved, most flown, and most profitable airline.
- Mission: The mission of Southwest Airlines is a dedication to the highest quality of customer service delivered with a sense of warmth, friendliness, individual pride, and company spirit.

Take a bit of time and start with your why. Do you want to solve a problem in your lifetime? Show your kids you can do it? Provide for your family? Impact your community? These are just a few examples to inspire you. We all have a different why and different motivations. There is no right or wrong answer to this. No one ever needs to see your why. It's for you. To keep you going on those days when all you want to do is quit when you experience failure, or when you feel helpless.

Once you have your why, think about your mission and vision. What is the impact you want to have with your business? Where do you see it going?

I have shared examples from huge corporations as we know them and it's easier to see their missions and values in action due to their sizes. But remember that you are starting your path as a tiny business owner. Don't let the hugeness of these companies intimidate you. You are doing this exercise to help you understand how to make decisions, what to do with your time and to navigate the direction you are going. You do not have to be saving the world or declaring a mission that feels impossible.

Revisiting Your Why, Mission, and Vision Annually

Your why is not like getting your driver's license. It's not something you have to do once and then hopefully never have to go through again. It's something that will most likely evolve over time. Have grace with yourself and avoid adding the pressure to make a perfect purpose statement. It's only for you, to help you make sure you are doing the work which aligns with your values.

If you decide next week to rewrite it, no problem, if you don't want to do it, that's fine. Do not let it hold you back from taking the next steps. No one is going to give you a test on your why. Get something down on paper and keep taking action!

A few years ago, I experienced burnout. I was the last person to realize this. After a year or so when I finally became aware of it, I realized something interesting. I realized that my purpose had evolved and that I was still running a business towards a past metric of success, and a past mission and vision. It made me feel like I was constantly missing something. I was feeling a bit empty inside and incredibly frustrated with my work. I kept trying to get involved in new projects and community service to fix this unnamed feeling. I, however, couldn't shake it. It wasn't until I sat down one day at the end of December to review the year and finally thought about my why, that things started to fall into place.

I realized I was no longer driven by my past motivations and it was creating a great deal of personal unrest. I thought about what I was currently driven by and what I wanted to pursue. It wasn't instant, but over the next few weeks, I made the decision to shut down my company that I had spent 16 years building. This caused an interesting reaction in my own little business community as my peers were angry that I was closing a "successful business". I have no idea why it caused them anger towards me, but I'm sure the answer was wrapped up in each of their own metrics of success.

I created a year-long plan. But the minute I made the decision to close, it was like a massive boulder had been lifted from my shoulders and I decided to make the move faster. No decision had ever felt so wonderful than to release me from a business that no longer aligned with what I wanted to do with my life, with my why.

I realized that I had been trying to force the business to evolve into something that would fit with what had shifted with my changed mission, vision, and idea of success. Not only was it not working, but it was making me more frustrated, as it felt so forced. I am thankful that I was able to close the business quickly and that my exit plan worked well enough to provide the cushion I needed to move onto the next business.

This is why it is important to review your why, your mission and your vision annually. I realized that it's ok to change my mind. That I may not always be in alignment with what I had once thought. I also realized that it's ok to close a successful business that I had built and move on. The world did not end, no one was harmed, and I was more fulfilled in the next business I created.

A Note on Being "Qualified" To Start a Business

Are you qualified to start a business? Yes. You are. I am asked this often, but there is no degree, certification, or piece of paper that will make one iota of difference about you being qualified to start a business. You may have specific tests and requirements to practice at something, like law, or medicine, or therapy. There are of course certain things that require specific degrees and certifications (well, one would hope. There have been an insane amount of grifters in history who have practiced medicine and law with zero qualifications!) but to own a business where others do the practicing of law, medicine or therapy, you do not. You simply need to go through the legal steps of business formation.

Will an MBA help your business succeed? No. In fact, the curriculum of MBA programs has little to do with very small businesses (the SBA deems this as 50 employees or less) and nothing to do with tiny businesses (my own term, meaning 5 and under employees). Save yourself the massive investment of time and money.

What about certifications? Bluntly, they have become a lucrative way for educational institutions to make more money. Cynical, perhaps, but schools are businesses too. If you are coming from corporate America, you may have been trained to collect certifications as you climbed the ladder. They do mean something in the corporate world. But for a tiny business, no one cares one bit. What people do care about is customer service, peer recommendations (ratings and reviews), if you are solving their problem, and how you make them feel. Honestly, you don't even have to have great products and services, if you make your clients and customers feel amazing about doing business with you and are addressing their needs, that's all that matters.

Rarely do people decide to use a service or product based on the certifications the tiny business owner holds. And the sad reality is, most of the time when we visit businesses where degrees and certifications are required, such as doctors, lawyers, therapists, we just want to know where they went to school and see that they graduated. For those of us who are not in law or health, well, no one has ever asked me where I went to school, what my degree was in, or what my GPA was. I doubt they care.

Certificates with tiny business owners tend to be largely ego-based or an attempt at stopping impostor syndrome. They make us feel better about being "qualified", and help with confidence. But they are not needed. No one cares that you are certified in excel, they just want to know that you can use it well for what you are providing them.

A few years ago, I was approached by venture capitalists for my jewelry brand. To this day, I have no idea why, I must have ended up randomly on a list somewhere or that degree that helps me build lovely websites was in play. Anyway, for about three days, I researched the firm and called people to ask for advice. After a few nice conversations catching up with friends and asking questions, I made a decision and never gave it another thought. I moved on, confident in my decision to decline.

Why? Well first, I reached out to people whom I trust and asked what VC backed companies looked like (another story for another day) and then I realized that me, as an art school graduate and the designer/owner, well, I would be kicked out faster than I could blink. In my research, I considered all the possibilities to make the scenario work. I even thought, well what if I got an MBA? But after reaching out to more people, I quickly realized that it would do me no good, I would not learn the skills in getting an MBA for what I was looking for and it would not have a good ROI. Was it the right decision to make? I still think so. I would have gone back to school, spent a ton of money and time to receive a degree simply to prove that I was qualified. Would I have been more qualified? No. But, I'm pretty happy to save the money and the time.

Do not rush out and collect degrees or certifications thinking it will help you start your business. Instead, get out there and start talking to people and build relationships with a network of people who will know, like, and trust you, ultimately, passing on the word about what you do.

Sum It Up:

- Defining what success means to you will help you determine your goals and the work you need to do each week and day.

- Your vision, mission, and values will help you stay on track and keep yourself motivated to do the work.
- Reviewing your definition of success, your vision, mission, and values each year will prevent burnout.

Chapter 3:

Finding the Problem Your Solving

Okay, so you're talented. That's great. You have decided to start a business. Even better, I'm so proud of you, that's awesome. That alone probably got you some attention and inquiries into how to work with you. Maybe it got you some sales. That's all fine and good. Now going forward, let's approach business with a bit more strategy so you can consistently profit and have a cash flow. Cash flow, as we have learned, is essential to staying in business.

In the early years as a jewelry designer, when I would do exercises about the problem I was solving with my business, I was always a bit annoyed. I made jewelry. My customers, who called themselves "Trouties", enjoyed accessorizing with handmade baubles. However, as business grew and I began working with brand strategists, I began to understand why it was important to dig a bit deeper and look deeper into why they would choose my jewelry. Spoiler alert, the more it became about solving a problem for my customers, the more successful I became.

There are many people out there who would read this and think, why on earth would you start a business without knowing the problem you are solving? Well, the answer is...complicated. Talented, tiny business owners often start a business around their skill(s). There is most likely a need for their skill and their skill is a solution to a problem, but they don't approach it that way. Talented people tend to come to business differently than someone who approaches starting a business by looking for a problem to solve. You know what you are good at and like to do, now we need to make sure that there are things you can do, make, or sell that people will pay you money for.

Your business needs to solve a problem which people are not only experiencing but will pay to solve. Once you know what problems you are solving, you will need to communicate that you are solving that problem to the people having it, essentially, marketing. Solving a problem is the root of your business, which means knowing the problems you are solving and communicating how you will solve them is the key to the success of your business.

Our goal is to identify problems and offer solutions in a clear and thoughtful manner. This also is important when you want to add something to your business, be it a new service or a new product, or a new revenue stream. Approach adding future revenue streams by setting out to identify additional problems for your existing clients and offering solutions. If you're talented, but you're struggling to get clients and customers, it may be because you have not identified the problem you're solving or you're not communicating to your audience what the problem you are solving is.

If you are talented, you are lucky to already know the answer to the half of the equation or what to build your business around, the what you are good at doing half. As I said, we're coming at this a little backward. Now the other half of that equation is what is needed or what the problem is that these skills are solving. Some people may approach starting a business as looking for what problems need to be solved. And then they move onto figuring out what their skills are that can be used to solve this problem. We're not those people.

If you are starting a business around a specific skill, let's say practicing law or graphic design, I'm assuming you like to use these skills. The key to having a business that you enjoy putting your energy into and that you want to tell everybody about is to match your skills with the problem you want to solve.

So how do we identify the problem to solve? Well, start broad and then work towards a more specific niche. We're constantly hearing experts talking about niching down. This is what it means: it's that you are going to focus on an extremely specific thing. We'll take the lawyer as an example. Lawyers do not practice all types of law at once; they select one and build their practice around that. It may be family law, corporate law, or personal injury. That is an example of a niche within a field. You also can have a niche within a client base. A graphic designer may choose to specialize in working with women, or with doctors' offices, or with enterprise clients. Now as a talented person, I understand that this can be overwhelming to think about as there are so many ways to decide on a niche. Remember that you can always change it, this is simply a place to focus.

During the 16 years I was a jewelry designer and maker. I was running a company around my skill of being a designer, and niched down further and further over the years. As I mentioned at the start of this chapter, when I first started working on this exercise, I thought, I make jewelry, full stop. But then I realized that in order to successfully market myself, I had to get a little bit deeper than that. When it came down to it, I had to think about why I was doing it, to begin with.

When I first started making jewelry, I was in high school, in a small boarding school of 200 kids in New York. I started making jewelry with friends in our dorm, to alleviate boredom. But then it was because in the mid-nineties silver chain jewelry was all the rage. Think Tiffany's Elsa Peretti Necklaces and the Cartier Love Lock Bracelet. It's what everybody was designing.

It's what everybody was wearing. I did not want to wear it. I wanted to wear big, bold, colorful designs. I started making my own jewelry because without even understanding at 14, I was solving my own problem.

When I got to college, I started in architecture school but quickly applied to the art school where I studied computer graphics, which was both in the art school and the engineering school. I found that jewelry making was once again solving my own problem, which was that I needed to unwind from all that technical work. Making jewelry, playing with the colors, using my hands to put things together, did just that.

I was wearing most of the jewelry I made, and it was attracting attention. When I was in the local boutiques, I started to be asked if I would sell what I made to the store. Apparently, I was not the only person who was craving fun, colorful, and big jewelry. About five years later, I started a business where I officially and professionally designed and sold fun, colorful, and big jewelry after I had been making it as a hobby for 12 years.

I started realizing that my audience was looking for fun, colorful and big jewelry that they could wear to work. They were not looking for jewelry to wear to formal evening things. They were not looking for the kind of jewelry that you put on and never take off, like engagement rings or religious icon necklaces. They were looking for something which showed their personality and created a statement. Some of these people worked in the professions where you usually would have to wear more conservative jewelry (like lawyers), but on their informal days, they were wanting to show a little flair.

The problem I was solving was not that women want to wear jewelry and need to buy it from someone. It became that I provided high-quality, handmade solutions for the women who wanted to wear colorful statement pieces to work.

If you already are in business, you may have come this far by simply having a skill and attracting clients around that skill through word of mouth. You also probably have a customer base of whom you can actually ask about things, as in call them up on the phone and talk to them. I know this sounds crazy, maybe scary. Especially, if you have an online business or are not in a field where people speak on the phone. If you're an introvert, you may want to throw this book across the room. You're reading this, thinking, this is ridiculous, you want me to call these people up? They don't want to talk to me, and no one even answers the phone anymore. But guess what? They really would love to talk to you. And most of them are probably more extroverted than you think, and they don't have a problem with you calling at all.

This may seem like something that you do all the time. Either way, you can reach out to some of your best customers to have a phone call and share that you're trying to figure out a new product. Ask them what they like and what they don't like. I'll mention that the rule of thumb in creating products especially, is that people have no idea what they want, so don't take what they're saying at literal face value.

Ask questions you can write down the answers to. Talk to five customers and then look at where the patterns are. Look at where you're seeing the commonalities. If they all are, for example, wearing jewelry to the same type of events, or if you design a service and they all seem to be coming to you when they're having the same struggle, you're onto something. That's the problem that you're solving for them.

Even if you are an accountant where you can work with people no matter where they are in their business, what size business, even if they don't have a business, you'll start to notice that people are coming to you at certain pain points in their life. By talking to people, you can start identifying these pain points without guessing and figure out when you are solving the problems in their lives. This will enable you to create strategies.

At one point, in my jewelry business, I had lots of press. I wasn't necessarily looking for another problem to solve, but it fell into my lap. Because I noticed a pattern. I was getting emails from the spouses of my regular customers who were saying: "Do you have something more expensive? I really want to buy my wife a special present for our anniversary, as she loves your jewelry, but a $100 necklace is not going to do it. I want something that is a little fancier so I can treat her to something that she wouldn't treat herself to."

I ended up designing a luxe collection and what I found, was that not only did I solve the problem for these men, but as it turned out, women often were looking for a more luxurious, higher price point as well because they *did* want to treat themselves. They wanted to splurge when they got a promotion at work or had a special time to wear it approaching. With one of my very long-time customers, the first necklace she ever bought was when she graduated from an MBA program. There was a necklace that she decided to reward herself with upon graduation. And she did indeed buy it and even wore it with her cap and gown. And then proceeded to buy hundreds of necklaces over the next decade.

It's incredibly interesting when you start to play with different price points and levels of offerings. The psychology behind how people react to pricing with shopping is fascinating. Besides calling your people, the next step is to join Facebook groups or forums and just listen (well, read). If you find a forum or group around people that you know are your people, you can start to understand what their problems are by what they talk about.

You can even start talking to strangers. I love talking to strangers about things, especially when I used to design jewelry because I would wear it and then they would talk to me about it. But even now I will start talking to a random person about how I help talented, tiny business owners and they'll be like, who are those people? And then we start talking and I get a little bit of feedback right there. Even though they're not a customer, it helps to understand what people are looking for. And, in talking to strangers, they do become actual customers. Simply from striking up a conversation.

Then, of course, we have networking. I continuously stress the importance of networking. One of the big reasons is because it gives you a chance to talk to people. You get to constantly engage with a group of people who will begin to understand your business and who your people are. They may be your people, and they may also be a great sounding board. Use them to bounce new ideas off of!

Having conversations with your people, strangers, and your network is also a really great way to refine your messaging around the problem that you're solving. Back to that adding a new revenue stream, a new service, or a new product. Talking to your people really helps you figure out what you can add. Because if they're already your target demographic and you already know how to talk to them, why not solve another one of their problems?

Of course, once you've been talking to people and have identified problems, you'll need to determine if there is a market for the solution. If you're a talented person and you create a business around something that you're good at, occasionally you'll introduce something that no one will pay money for. Because the honest and sad truth is that there's not always a market for every solution that you're creating. You need to research and find out a few things. Does somebody else offer a similar solution? If they do, then you need to start looking at how you can be different in your solution. Can you be in a different niche? You want to be able to dominate a tiny area of the market.

You do not want to compete based on price and you should not get into the lower price game. That is a dangerous game that you will lose to big businesses with the ability to hire cheaper labor and manufacture. Think about what little particular area you can be in which will differentiate your business.

It could be a location if you have a brick-and-mortar. This is how businesses were created for centuries. People would say, "Look at this fantastic place I see on my vacation, I need to create this in my town." And then they would. With the internet, things are a little bit different, but you still can create different iterations depending on different niche markets.

Now, if no one is solving the problem, there's usually a good reason, like that nobody will pay for the solution or that the solution is simply too expensive to produce. But hopefully, somebody has tried to create a solution and if they have failed at it, you, thanks to the internet, will be able to see why. Look at why they've failed. If it has nothing to do with what the problem is, maybe they ended up having an illness in the family and had to step back. Or maybe they had a baby or had to care for a parent. If the reason it failed was due to a personal issue, then go for it. This may be a great problem to solve.

But if you see that 45 people have tried to solve this problem and every single one has failed because nobody was buying anything, this is not a problem that you want to solve. Learn from the mistakes of people before you.

Once you know your problem and you know who you're solving it for, your marketing will begin to have a storyline. Tell the story of the problem. Talk to who you're helping and let them know you'll solve their problem. You're defining the problem, then explain your solution. All in the voice your person relates to and identifies with. That's marketing.

In my current business, if I'm going to, let's say a networking event, and introducing myself in 30 seconds, I may say: "I help talented tiny business owners solve their problems from the technical to time management well past the startup phase."

When I sit down and have a one-on-one with people, I explain in better detail what I do. I talk about how I had owned a tiny business for a long time. I talk about how a few years into that business I faced this problem of being a talented person who did not necessarily know the business side of things and it took me a long time to figure it all out on my own. I wished that I had had people that I could talk to, people that I could ask the advice of, people that would not push me to strive to build a corporation on an enterprise level with a thousand employees.

I longed for people in the business education space who understood tiny businesses, who understood handmade, who understood lifestyle business. But that everybody who I kept talking to was not really understanding that and pushing me in another direction. That I felt frustrated. That there was so much information out there for new people but little out there for those of us in the middle years of tiny businesses. And that I became obsessed with solving this problem, which is why I ended up pivoting and going into what I'm doing now.

When I talk to people, they either immediately say, "Oh, that's me!" Or if it's not them, they still find it interesting and see the need for it. You want people to hear your message and say, "Oh, that's me!" Or introduce you to their friend who would say that. This is why understanding what the problem you are solving, who you're solving it for, and how to communicate your solution is so important. To get to the "Oh, that's me.", then to "Hey, that's my problem." And the very next thought would be, "Ah, you can help me solve it!"

Think about the problems you are solving for your people. Start to think about what it will look like to communicate what your solution is. Play around with it. You'll get there. I believe in you.

Sum It Up:

- Your business needs to be solving a problem to be successful.
- Talking to your clients, customers, peers, and even strangers can quickly help you understand what the needs are that your skills can solve.
- Once you know the problem, make sure that there is a market for the solution so that people will value what you offer and pay you for it.

Chapter 4:

Using Your Unique Skill Set

If I had pursued what I went to school for, I would have gone into something along the lines of designing and creating video games or at the time, Pixar movies. When I graduated, none of these appealed to me, so I opted not to pursue them. Were the skills I acquired for my degree a complete waste? Maybe on the surface, but the skills were pretty great to have in the late '90s, even if they were not being applied in an obvious way to my career. First, there was the ability to code, second to design websites, and third, to learn how to use any software in under 20 minutes. That last one is still one of my best superpowers and one I use to help hundreds of tiny business owners.

This skill set also led to my first business, which was custom website design for local small businesses (tiny, really) in the days before Etsy and social media. It quickly became clear that I had no interest in creating, or more astutely, maintaining websites for work. To recap, I had now rejected the two most obvious pursuits of my skill set. Did I mention I was a painting minor?

Well, I dabbled in pursuing painting professionally, and to fund that career, worked for a few years managing an artist's studio and briefly as a gallery assistant. Both jobs required a BFA, which delighted me, to put my degree to good use and made me realize that I did not want to paint for a living. Great. There were now many things I did not want to do.

But! All this time, I had still been making jewelry as a hobby, as I had for years in dorm rooms. I was getting better at it and was getting more and more interest from people about it. I decided to set up a website and build a shopping cart (a-ha! Those skills at work!). As I was an early user of Etsy, all of this attracted press early on. Thanks to my web design skills, I was always able to have an incredible, well-designed, and functioning website and it gave me a big leg up. Retailers and press were happy to take a chance on an Indie designer as the professionalism of my site made them trust me more.

Even today, decades later, I can build out things on websites that my competition would have to pay tens of thousands of dollars for. By using my unique skill set, I can set myself apart. As you decide your direction and as you grow, always keep in mind what your specific skills and talents are so that you can stack and use to your advantage.

Chances are, you know what you're good at doing. You may want to start a business around one thing you do well, like graphic design. That's awesome, I'm glad you're here. But perhaps you're sitting there thinking, that you have no idea what you do well or what direction to go in.

I'm going to remind you that no matter which lane you're in or if you're swerving back and forth between them, the most important thing to remember is that while certain skills are innate, most come from practice. What skills and talents are learned and honed by practice, intention, and putting in the work? If there is something that you enjoy doing, it's more likely that you'll want to keep going than if you are simply innately "good" at something.

We'll start with the things that you're good at and like to do. It's not necessarily in what you pursued, your education or work in the past. What is your version of making jewelry in your dorm room? It's about understanding where your skills are as well as which ones you want to nurture and grow. The areas where you want to learn more, and you are willing to do it repeatedly or are even excited about doing over and over again. Ideally, not a fleeting passion, but something like I had with jewelry, perhaps that you have been doing happily for years and years.

A reminder that the thing you do, such as making the jewelry, will be about 20% of the work you will do. The other 80% will be running and growing the business, so you will of course be doing plenty of other tasks, but you're beginning to get the idea.

You are not looking for what you are super passionate about, rather think about pursuing what you want to be focused on for years ahead. The slow burn, not the passing excitement.

Remember when I talked about being a painting minor? At one point, I really began to pursue it, and I got involved in the behind-the-scenes of it to understand the business side. I quickly understood that I wanted it to remain my passion. I did not want to have to spend all my time, energy, and focus on it. I did not want the pressure to paint every day; I did not want to force a value on the finished products and I absolutely did not want to constantly get rejected over what I painted. I was too passionate about it to make a living from it. I did, however, see that I did not have that passion for jewelry. I enjoyed the work. I wanted to get better at it, it was interesting to me. And I was right, I happily made jewelry for a living for the next 16 years, and I had been making it as a hobby for 10 years before that. Painting, however, fizzled from my passions and was replaced by new things.

So how do you choose? I enjoy a good list. I also find that there is a lot of power in journaling. The trick that makes me really open up in journals is that when the book is full, I throw it out. No pressure. No one ever will read the mess contained in the pages. However, your best process is best for you. Meditation, long walks, being in the water of any kind, talking it out with a good friend or all your friends. Any way you like to think and make decisions, go for it. Think about what the things are that you really enjoy showing up for. What is an area where you could research and do work every day? What could you talk to people about endlessly and want to solve problems around it?

The problem-solving aspect may be a big part of it. Have you encountered an issue, a roadblock, or a friction point where you want to make it so no one else goes through it? Understanding the problem you are solving may be the first step towards knowing what you want your business to be around. You can also figure out the skills you need later. When I was changing careers, I knew I wanted to talk about business. I knew that the problem I wanted to solve was that in all the years I was a tiny business owner, that I could not find much support or education for businesses with 5 or fewer employees.

I had no idea what a business that solved that problem would look like though. I did a lot of thinking, and I got myself out there immediately. I started with consulting, passed through a brief coaching phase, and kept pushing to discover how to solve the problem I had. I talked to hundreds of people to understand if they had this problem and what the solutions would be. I finally realized after I started to show up every day and gather my people, that I was really aiming to educate.

It was not a straight path to that realization. I had a FB group of 500 people gathered before I understood that my people were talented, tiny business owners. It took a pandemic to make me realize how much I enjoyed teaching them. From the first consulting client (who I did charge), to when I understood that I wanted to educate, it was about 18 months.

By that time, I had started to build a book of clients through consulting, speaking, creating a weekly podcast, blogging, and creating weekly live videos. I was showing up, I was doing the work all the while I was figuring it out. Don't be afraid to commit and go for it. And don't fear charging from day one. You are in business to make a profit. You are not here to work for free. You can change anything you set up at the beginning later. You can wake up one day and realize that you hated the work you were doing in the business you had created, grown, and built for 16 years. There is no one to stop you from shutting a door and opening another.

What are the things that you want to put the work in for the next few years? What are the things that your friends are always pointing out that you're great at? I kept being told by people that I was good at taking in a vast amount of often complicated information, distilling it down, and communicating it well to people. Which in hindsight is teaching, but that took some time for me to see.

Where are the areas that people are always coming to you

for help? They will not all be areas you want to work in, but it's a good place to begin. Don't feel weird if you have skills you really don't want to create a business around, keep searching for the things you want to do, not just can do.

What Do You Really Dislike?

Now that we have talked about what the things are that you'd like to show up for every day, let's talk about what you want to avoid. I will begin this section with a reminder that there are some parts of owning a tiny business that is not for all personalities. And that's fine! Why force it? My husband, Adam for example, loves to work with a team. He wants to be surrounded by people all day long and he despises working alone. A few years ago, he had a friend with a tech startup who asked if he would be a sales rep for the company in Austin. He could do it as a side job and it would only be for a few months to test the market. Like starting a business, the work required that Adam be alone most of the time, create his own schedule, and his own metrics to measure his successes. He hated every minute of it. It was a great lesson as it made us both realize that Adam loves to work for a big corporation. He's great at it, the culture suits him well. His friends are mostly self-employed and give him a hard time about building a business for someone else, but it's what he loves to do. He gets so much of what he needs from it, the structure, the systems, and that team. No shame in the corporate game!

As Adam realized, there are some things that you simply may not find in the land of the self-employed. This section is a good place to pay attention to if you are having doubts about how much you want to start a business. If you are naming all the things that you dislike doing and they are major aspects of owning a business, there are plenty of other options for work that you may enjoy more. Working for a self-employed person is a great path if you like some aspects but not all. As we talk about tiny businesses, those 5 or fewer employees are a huge part of the business world, there are millions of them that you could go work for. If you love let's say, everything about tiny businesses except the stress, the money worry, or the responsibility — being one of those 5 employees can be an incredibly fulfilling path.

Take some time to have a real talk with yourself about the things that you put off and never want to do. There are some things, like bookkeeping, well, I think many of us who own businesses don't want to do that, that we can assume most of us won't enjoy. It's probably the first to get outsourced, so that is not a red flag. But if you really don't like talking to people and are setting out to be a consultant or coach of some sort, that will become problematic.

Make a list of the things you don't like to do. Then have a hard look at it and decide which are the non-enjoyable tasks, and which are things you never want to do, like Adam with working alone.

A note about outsourcing. Corporate people love to talk about how in their work, they outsource to the best. And then they smugly tell you that you should do the same with every aspect of your business. This may be one of my greatest pet peeves in life. Yes, they have budgets to adhere to, but they are budgets with bank accounts behind them, often large ones. There is plenty of money to pay all this talent, and many incentives to offer the talent to make them want to do work for them. If you are a tiny business owner with no funding, you have to earn the extra income to pay people for any outsourcing.

The corporate people are right about one thing though, you don't want to hire hacks to do the work, you want to outsource to highly skilled people. Well, guess what, highly skilled people are expensive, as they can and should be. It will not be an option at all for a few years to outsource unless you have money to spend. Maybe some help here and there, but the first year especially, it will be all you.

I tell you this so you understand the reality of what you are getting into and so you understand what needs to be done. Not only is money necessary for outsourcing, but you also need to have a deep understanding of the work you plan to outsource. If you spend a year doing all the things and increasing your earnings, you will be in a fantastic position to outsource appropriately as you grow. Look again at your list. Will you be willing to learn to do these things (like the bookkeeping) and do them for at least a year? Are you ok with that?

What Will People Pay You For?

Now that you have a better understanding of what you like to do and what you don't want to have to do, let's get into if people will pay you to do or create the things you like to do. And if they will pay you enough to make it worth you doing it.

The truth that many people like to avoid is that even if someone has managed to make a living from doing something, it does not mean that it will be easy for you to do the same. Unless it's the only thing you like to do, you may want to stay away from some areas. There are things to do related to what you enjoy, but the thing itself may be prohibitive due to it being so hard to make money at. Knitting comes to mind. Good yarn is expensive. Even the fastest knitters spend more than a few hours on creating a sweater. Add in the costs of operating a business and you are soon approaching paying yourself sweatshop wages. Now selling knitting patterns…that's a whole different ball game and a great strategy!

You need to understand a bit of the market and "what the market will bear" before you dive in blindly and build a business around something which is doomed to fail. According to the Bureau of Labor Statistics, around 20% of businesses fail in the first year. 30% fail in the second year. 50% fail after 5 years and 70% after 10 years. Only 25% of businesses make it to 15 years.[8]

Now I would argue that many of those who don't get to the 15-year mark are simply wanting to move on to something new by then. As someone who got past the 15-year mark and just didn't want to do it anymore, even though the business itself was great. I'd also be curious to see if "fail" is synonymous with "closed". At any rate, when you own a business, you are fighting an uphill battle from the beginning. You want to set yourself up for success as much as possible.

I'm about to get controversial now, but you do not need a business plan. Unless you need funding, they are mostly a waste of time (with the exception to the marketing plan part which will constantly evolve, and we'll get to later). All a business plan will get you to do is guess at the future based on the confirmation biased research you do. Instead of spending hours making up a guess at the future, you need to make sure you can make a living at what you want to do.

The first thing is to research if people actually get paid for what they want to do. Does anyone find value in this thing you want to work in? It does not have to be a vast amount of people, but enough to create a niche market. If you are solving a problem

8 Business failure rates are consistent across industries, and no, restaurants do not fail at a greater rate: https://www.sba.gov/sites/default/files/Business-Survival.pdf

that no one has solved, investigate why no one else has solved it. If 25 people have tried and failed, research why. It could be that they all realized that it is prohibitory expensive to do so. Or that people like the idea but won't pay for it. Competition is actually good when you are researching, you can always put your own spin on something, but if no one is paying anything for what you want to offer, it will be hard to build a business around it.

The next step is to make sure that it's possible to make the amount of money you need to make and have room for growth. The best example is with trading hours for dollars. If you are in a service industry, anything from being a lawyer to doing taxes to consulting, you will have to spend time with people or do things for them in a set amount of time that you are charging for. A smart rule of thumb is that the hour you bill for will be two hours of work. That would mean if you work a 40 hour week, that you would be billing clients for 20 hours and the rest of the time will be operating the business. This is an average of course, and you can work as many hours as you'd like. But understand that if your billable rate has to be below a certain dollar amount then you may not be able to even earn enough. There are reasons why many in the service industries have high hourly rates. Once an office and staff come into play, that hour of time is responsible for a great deal of overhead.

The most logical way is to figure out what you want or need

to make during a year, and then start doing the math. Divide by hours, or product cost, or whatever your COGS (cost of goods sold) is, allow 25% for taxes, another % for overhead and see where you are.

Now if you are like I am, and you have created a business of offerings that are not unheard of, but not common to the audience, you have to test how much people will realistically pay. I, like many knowledge businesses, offer a variety of services and products from 1:1 consulting, to downloadable worksheets. When I am thinking of introducing a new offering or removing something, I play around with the idea that if I sell this many 1:1 hours, this many worksheets, this many workshops, my income for the week would be X. If I change the numbers around, it will look like Y. Once you get a few revenue streams in place you can begin to think about all of the options, but until then, keep it simple and start with one number or an average if you have products.

Do some research to see if people will pay you for what you want to be the staple of your business. Be sure that you can charge enough and have room to grow. We will talk about pricing later, but this quick exercise will make sure you are not setting yourself up to fail and that you have a shot of being in the 80% that makes it through the first year!

Building a Business Around You

A word on the questions about how smart it is to build a business around you and your skills. Will it make the business sellable? No, probably not. Some would argue that you are just creating a job then, and not a business. I would counter with creating a job that you love and find interesting every day, and perhaps having the freedom, aka flexibility to pick up kids from school or pursue other endeavors is usually worth it.

The failure rate for businesses, as we've discussed, is incredibly high. There are 30.7 million small businesses in the US, which are 99.9% of US-based businesses. Small businesses are classified as having under 500 employees or less.[9] 75% of these are tiny, at 5 employees or under.

You have a good chance of starting a tiny business and really enjoying what you do while earning a solid income that can support you and your family. Keep in mind that in 2020, 75% of freelancers reported that they made the same *or more* than compared to when they were employed[10]. Not bad for a "job" you've created out of nothing.

Today, there are approximately 3,500 publicly traded

---

9 The most recent small business stats: https://cdn.advocacy.sba.gov/wp-content/uploads/2019/04/23142719/2019-Small-Business-Profiles-US.pdf

10 Upwork has a great annual study on Freelancers: https://www.upwork.com/press/releases/new-upwork-study-finds-36-of-the-us-workforce-freelance-amid-the-covid-19-pandemic

companies[11], about half of what there were in 1996 and a good deal of these are small. No matter what, it's realistic to not aim to create an enterprise-level business, which I tend to lump all together and refer to as "Google". How many employees does Google, or rather its parent company Alphabet have? As of June, 2021, they have reached 135,601 employees.[12] Which gives you a 0.02% chance of getting hired by them, never mind starting a similar business yourself.

That's all exciting and a bit dramatic, but it makes my point. So much of the information about creating companies pushes us in the direction of the giants, the top of the enterprise level. Why? Because it's a good story. It's sexy, it sells books. Even Jim Collins, the author who wrote Good To Great among others, said in an interview on the Tim Ferriss podcast (ep 483)[13] that he set out to teach small business, and still really loves those best, but his writing about enterprise businesses was simply paid more attention to and made him more money.

Creating a DBA around just you, doing the work that you find interesting and exciting can be an incredibly smart move. Betting it all to hope for being one of the most well known CEOs, like Elon Musk, well, if you want to go that route, we'll all cheer

11 Wilshire Index: https://www.wilshire.com/indexes/wilshire-5000-family/wilshire-5000-total-market-index

12 All about Alphabet: https://fortune.com/company/alphabet/fortune500/

13 You can listen to the episode here: https://tim.blog/2020/11/30/jim-collins-returns/

for you, but know that you can own an incredibly profitable business and live your life as a tiny business owner as well.

Not starting because we feel daunted by not being big is all your mindset. Start small, and you may just love where you end up!

Side Hustles

What do you do if you want to do something that is not going to make enough to support you, but you would still like to pursue it? Well, that is the original idea behind side hustles. It used to be that people would have a side job to make ends meet or to pursue something they enjoy, but not give up the security of a full-time job. Then it became an obsessive concept labeled side hustles and got a bit weird, but the idea is a great one. You can even have a side hustle for your business. Side hustles do not have to become these big things on their own, they can remain super tiny.

I have a friend and client who is a full-time, residential Realtor. She loves her business; she also loves to bake. Where she lives, you can get your kitchen zoned for a cottage industry business and have your kitchen be commercial. The one caveat is that you cannot sell more than $22k a year of product and the food must be sold to go. It works well in this case, as the two businesses work well together. All the baked goods can be made, without having to rely on the income or on her eating them all.

This could be a great path for those of you who have creative pursuits in mind and do not want to spend all your time making. Or people who want to monetize a blog or podcast, but not make it a full-time endeavor. It can be a side hustle or a revenue stream of your business. Both are fine ways to do it and what you'll read in this book will still apply to you.

There is no right or wrong way to start a business. You never have to grow it bigger than a 12.2k (over 12.2k denotes it's not a hobby according to the IRS[14]) a year business or you can shoot for making the next Google. It's all up to you and what you want to create.

"Where we're going, there are no roads."

- Dr. Emmett Brown, Back to the Future

Sum It Up:

- Your skills are a collection of what you have picked up with experience, education and practice. Your leg up in a market may be due to a skill from a previous industry.
- Not all skills are created equal in people's minds. Understand what people will pay for and how to explain the value of your skills.

14 Determine if you have a hobby or a business: https://www.irs.gov/newsroom/hobby-or-business-irs-offers-tips-to-decide

- Forget what you've heard about building "a business, not a job" (those words are how sketchy business models get you to buy in). It's ok if it's centered around you and your skills. It's also ok if it never becomes full time.

Chapter 5:

Interacting with Your People

Most likely, if you are reading this book, you came to the table knowing exactly what you want to do for work and now want to build a business around it. Great. The first step is to figure out where to hang your shingle. Either in real life or figuratively. And it can be a combo of both.

When I was a few years into my jewelry company, my stepfather at the time said something along the lines of, if I had to do it all over again, I would have built my business to look more like yours. Keeping a low overhead instead of creating so much of a physical presence. He's in an industry that, like many, is traditionally in person, but has evolved beautifully online. However, his operating costs are high. At the time of our conversation, he had a monthly overhead of around $30,000 which makes it so a ton of business needs to be done simply to break even. I had a studio in my home out of which I was able to have room to bring in help when I needed it, manufacture all of the jewelry, and fulfill orders.

Remember how we learned that business failures are largely contributed to lack of cash flow? The higher your overhead, the more cash you need to come through your bank account each month. The most important factor at the beginning is you are delivering what you have promised to your clients and customers. How that process looks can vary greatly from business to business. How will your business look?

When you start thinking about what your interaction with customers and clients will look like, the first thing to think about is how scrappy you want to be able to be. Do you want to self-fund the profits from the business as you grow? Commercial rental space often requires a multiple-year lease as well as a big deposit. You also will need to furnish, or even do construction on the space. You'll have to start off with a good amount of money and you'll have a big monthly bill hanging over your head if you do go this route. Ideally in this situation, you would have funds upfront to get you through the first year or so. You could use your savings, get help from friends and family. You could also get a loan.

This is the one area I will urge you to really sit on your decision before you jump. Talk to people who rent offices and are in a similar work environment and see how they feel about it. Many people who rent expensive office spaces find themselves a few months in never working there and regretting the 5-year lease. Start as small as you can until you outgrow your free or inexpensive situation. Phil Knight of Nike worked out of his tiny apartment for years before he leased an office!

You also want to be thinking both about how your ideal working environment looks like to present your work and interact with clients. Is it you firing up your computer and putting yourself out there as a business-to-business (B2B) service to your network? Great, you can start right now, get on social media and declare that you are taking clients. You don't even have to leave your kitchen table. Is it you hand-making art and selling it? Excellent, you can easily open an Etsy shop and create in a spare bedroom, your dining room, or your garage. Is it going on your own to provide salon services? Wonderful, you can start by making house calls, like Alli Webb of Drybar who made house calls for ages after she left her salon job of 15 years. She ended up building a hair empire. But that, as she is the first to point out, was thanks to her brother and husband who ran the business side. She also had worked for a major fashion designer and did PR in the past, so that is another huge leg up. She is by no means a tiny business, but she did start out that way![15]

This is a great time to remind you of something many people who start tiny businesses fail to remember. If you start with the

15 Listen to a great interview with Alli Webb on How I Built This: https://www.npr.org/2017/01/09/508578306/drybar-alli-webb

simplest and least expensive way of doing something and get bigger as you grow, your chance of success will be much greater. First, because you are proving that there is a market for your product or service. Perhaps there's not a market beyond your tiny business, but at least prove that people will buy what you are offering.

Second, the only way you are going to get money as you grow, such as a loan, is to prove your business track record or offer something valuable as equity, like your house. Starting a business with zero business experience and your house on the line, well that is just not the kind of stress most of us want to take on.

If you start to read business profiles of most of the companies started today, you know that a good deal of them started with the owner living on a friend or family member's couch, making zero money, trying to get an idea to take off in a tiny way. Look at the Airbnb guys. Brian Chesky and Joe Gebbia started out in debt and then took 2 years to see any traction. They designed and sold breakfast cereals to raise funds for the business. Granted, they too ended up with a huge company, but they still had to start somewhere.[16]

Why is this important to remember? Because you need to make sure you have people to sell to. You need to make sure

16 Brian Chesky tells the story wonderfully on the Masters of Scale podcast: https://mastersofscale.com/brian-chesky-handcrafted/

there is an actual desire for what you have. It can be a tiny group at first, and for some businesses, it never even has to be that large of a number, which Kevin Kelly has famously shown us in 1000 True Fans blog post.[17]

Many, many business owners start with a false delusion that if you do market research and have a business plan, that the people will come. But that is sadly, not reality. You can plan all you want, but if what you have doesn't catch and start selling, you may be sitting there in a big empty space, having no idea how to pay for it.

Slight rant, but I really don't understand why the SBA instructs the order it does for how to start a business. The very first thing you should do, before you spend any money, is making sure that you can get someone to pay you for what you offer. Then start to think about how you want to interact and where you want to be set up. You may have no idea! If you have a business that is non-traditional, you may not know at all what it will look like (and that's ok too).

The entire time I had a jewelry business, people told me to open a store that I could design in the back and then come out when people came in. Well, I knew friends with shops over the years and quite frankly, if I had time to get to work in the back, my store would not be successful. And, knowing my work style,

17 Read the revised and original 1000 True Fans posts here: https://kk.org/thetechnium/1000-true-fans

I would be incredibly frustrated to be interrupted all the time. For a brick-and-mortar store to do well, it takes a ton of work. We only have so many hours in the day, I did not want to spend so many of mine on a storefront. Especially as a secret introvert who prefers to work alone and in silence all day. Knowing what my idea of success looked like, what my skills were, what I liked to do, and what my work environment should be, stopped me from making that mistake! This is why it's so important to understand yourself and your business!

The second example is in what I do know. When I first closed the jewelry company, I was not really sure what I wanted to do. Only that I knew I wanted to help a specific demographic of business owners. But I was not entirely sure what that looked like yet. The only thing I did know was that I had to make it so they could reasonably afford what I offered. I did a bit of consulting for tiny business owners, which led me to think I wanted to go into business coaching. This quickly became something I did not want to do. But up to that point, everything seemed to be 1:1 work with clients. If you recall back to the last example when I shared that I was a secret introvert? Well, that means 1:1 training is exhausting for me and not what I want the basis of my business to be.

I kept testing, talking to people, making a little more income each week from 1:1 coaching, and putting more money into the business. In what I do, most of my overhead is in fees to belong to organizations, associations, and attending events; books; software (so much technology), and showing up. I say showing up because the cost of blazers, makeup, and gas adds up. It's the truth. The point of this rambling is that when I started what I'm doing now, I had plans and research to prove there was a need in the market, but only by applying it out in the real world, was I able to cater to what my people really wanted.

From the day I started to consult to the day I started understanding what the business needed to be and hit the target with my positioning, led to me finally making an income I could live on, grow the business and rely on, took about a year and a half. Until then, as I have discussed, I was in a lucky situation where I had seed money from closing my previous business, but I did not have enough to sign a 2-year lease or build out a brick and mortar and still have that grace period to figure it all out. And oh yeah, 2 months after I did figure it all out, a global pandemic hit and turned every business upside down for at least a little bit.

Now that you have a few real-life examples, I hope you feel a bit more secure in understanding that you don't have to know from day one where you want to base your business. But to be on the safe side, you should stay scrappy as long as you can. And that you can start with a membership to a networking group and a free zoom account and be open for business as you figure it out.

Where Will You be Virtually?

These days, almost all businesses need to have something online. Where should you begin and what do you need to focus on?

To start, you can use your name, but as in the legal chapter, I will encourage you to also have a separate business name legally, even if you are using your name for the business. For now, try and buy the domain for your own name and make sure you have it saved on the big social media accounts. Facebook, Instagram, Pinterest, Twitter and LinkedIn, YouTube, SnapChat and TikTok. You do not need to use them, but you should have them to keep anyone else from getting them. If your name is taken, you can add in a middle name or use "Ms" or "Mr" at the beginning. Get creative! This past year I finally, after 20 years of someone holding it over me, was able to buy my domain name. And for the usual low fee, not the extortion they had been trying to get me to submit to for two decades. Although it feels great to own it, my name on Instagram had been grabbed up before I even was on there, and I was on there early. In order to be consistent across all channels, I went with @MsSierraBailey. It's not perfect, but it's the same on everything and people find me with no problem.

If you are already on anything besides Facebook for personal use and your name does not match on them all, research how to rename your profiles so you can lead people to @yourname as one consistent thing. It will make life easier in the long run. If you already know your business name, do all of this with your business name. You will most likely not be using both names on the social channels. You will mark whichever one you do not use for social as private and never use it. But you want to make everything the least confusing as possible, so it's good to own it. In the description of the account you don't use, fill in your info including your lnk.bio or Linktree in the URL, and say something like, "I use my @thenameIuse for all posts, come follow along there!" in the description. You can look at @ doersshakersmakers on Instagram for inspiration.

Once you have your name, you can decide if you want to have a website, or a landing page set up. You don't need to do this, but at the very least, investigate using something like lnk. bio[18] or link tree to use in your social profiles for people to contact you or see examples of your work. Ideally, you would set up a free email list account (like Mailchimp) and have a link to signing up for your email list in there as well, but you can hold off on that. The point is that you can get creative and at a low cost if you are strategic.

18 https://lnk.bio/, https://linktr.ee/

To begin, select no more than three social media places to focus your time. Start posting at least once a week about what you are doing or wanting to do. Nothing grand and crazy, not by shouting that you are a Business with a capital B, just starting to gently put yourself out there. Invite those who support you to follow you and start engaging. Look up people in the industry where your work will be and follow them to see how they use the platforms. Get into the habit of posting at least once a week on all 3 platforms. In the restaurant world, this is called a soft opening. You want to make sure you know what you are doing and get your name, branding, and offerings nailed down before you go too wild with marketing. It gives you time to figure it out and less to change as you evolve. You now have the start of your online presence!

Sum It Up:

- Start small and grow as you go.
- You'll need a place either virtually or IRL where you will interact with your clients/customers. From online store fronts to coffee shops to a brick n' mortar space. This will depend on what your business is.
- With your social media presence, the same idea of staying scrappy still applies. Keep it simple at the beginning, claim your space, and start slow.

Chapter 6:

Making Space for Work

You know how some girls dreamed of their weddings when they were little? I dreamed of my office. Not to say you can't dream of both, I just always really liked office supplies, and big desks. The first piece of grown-up furniture I ever bought was a massive, antique teachers' desk. Twenty-something years later, and I still love it. I'm working at it right now while writing this book. My love for office supplies burns so strong that they have become a big part of my current office decor. No coincidence there.

When I was little and playing 'office', I never wanted anyone in or near my workspace. This also still holds true and I prefer to work in total silence. I read Steven King's memoir, *On Writing*, and my biggest takeaway was the shock I felt that he wrote while blaring music. As Amy Pohler would say, "great for him, not for me." *My* ideal office looks like me alone in a quiet room with lots of office supplies and large tables to spread out on. What is yours?

Do you have space in your home you can dedicate to your

work? I'm not even talking about an office or guest room. We're talking about a little space where you can leave your work in progress, where you can be on zoom meetings without stress, where you can focus.

As I am writing this in the middle of a global pandemic, we have to take into account that you may not have public options like were once available. Especially those of us with service-based, online businesses, where we assume that we need zero space, that our cell phone, a laptop, and a place to sit are enough. But realistically, running even a business with zero physical needs ends up requiring you to sometimes need a table to work at or a place to store some things.

At least with the cloud, we don't have much paperwork anymore, but you still may need a printer, perhaps a tripod, a camera, or some notebooks, and maybe 300 pens (just me on that one? I doubt that…I see you my fellow office supply nerds.). Some of you may be thinking that this is ridiculous if you live in a spacious house, but for those of you in tight quarters, think of where you will dedicate a little space for yourself. Houses and apartments built in the '90s and later, often have huge closets. You can absolutely squeeze a tiny office in a closet if you're creative with it! Have you seen all the great tiny office inspiration on Pinterest? I love them and I've made a whole board of them. Most of them are made of an armoire or a small coat closet and are so creative. You open the door, there is your desk, pull the chair out and you have a place to both work and stash your stuff. Amazing!

If you sell products, either one you make (then you'll have raw materials and tools to store as well) or ones you purchase to resell, you will need to make sure you have room for all of these things as well as shipping materials and a place to handle fulfillment. You may avoid some of this if you choose to dropship and or use fulfillment, but if you are unsure of the specifics at this point, keep all of this in mind. And make sure you ask yourself, do you have space to grow?

The last thing to consider about workspaces is noise. Some people thrive in a noisy and chaotic environment. If you are not one of those people, be aware of your surroundings. Personally, I find coffee shops to be incredibly distracting. And co-working spaces end up with me talking to everyone. Neither of those options is conducive to my working. Are you able to work and focus in your workspace at home? If you are on Zoom often, will it remain relatively quiet (with earphones) and uninterrupted space?

Now you have an idea of what your working environment needs to look like. Great, now make a little space for yourself!

Sum It Up:

- Think about more than what your ideal work space looks like. Do you feel like you can relax and get things done?
- You'll need designated space to keep the things you use for your business. This does not need to be grand or intricate, but you will need at the very least a drawer and a place where you can have quiet when needed.

Chapter 7:

You'll Never Feel Ready to Start

My first attempt at a business was in the late '90s with photo imaging and website design. When I was in art school, I had a side gig with a local photographer/photo developing store (which is not even a thing anymore) doing digital restoration on photos. I restored old photos, created compilations between multiple photos, and removed or added things to photos. I still have no idea how that even happened. Really, I was thinking about it and thought, how did I start doing that? No memory of it whatsoever. At the time, I was in school full time and had a job, but that is how I roll, why not add more to the task list? The busier I am, the more I seem to take on.

When should you start your business? Or rather when will you be ready to begin? There is no right time. I mean really, that's all you need to know. But, will it convince you if you are stuck or paralyzed from getting going? Of course not! Most of the business owners I talk to who are doing well seem to have started in a similar way that I described in the last chapter, slow, scrappy, and open to change. It's served me well in my own businesses to ease in. I've now done it three times and once, it saved me from building a business around something I didn't want to own a business in.

Essentially, you are starting without being a business. You are telling a few people about what you are doing and then getting paid to do it. If you already work in the area you are starting a business in, it's about getting your first clients. You are testing not only your idea and the market, but if this is what you want to do.

After I graduated, I continued photo imaging work and designed websites for a few local small businesses. I worked as an assistant to a gallery owner and as an assistant to a painter and even got a solo show for myself. Within a few months, I knew that I did not want to do either the digital work or paint. But I was becoming more interested in people wanting my jewelry. Sometimes allowing yourself a test phase before you're ready can be the best thing you can do!

Don't Make a Big Deal Out of Starting

I not only suggest that you start in a low-key, under-the-radar way, but I don't want you to put a lot of pressure on yourself. Again, I will stress that perfection is not the goal here, it's to take action. To get out there and test your idea. See if you want to do the initial business, or if you want to adjust before you have invested a lot of money, time, or had resources created that now you won't need.

I know of many talented, tiny business owners who invest thousands of dollars into "starting" before they ever sell anything. They have had a $5,000 website built with fancy logos and photos. Then they set out to actually sell something and realized that what they were offering was not for them. Or that they were wrong about their target audience or any other of the dozens of things that can change in the beginning. By the time they launched, they had to scrap all of that time and money because things changed so much when they actually started the work.

Do not start with all your branding and materials before you sell things. This is an outdated way of starting a business. A name is a great place to start but avoid having a definition of what you do in the name and be open to change as you test.

You need to simply take action and begin. It's incredibly easy to get stuck in the planning, goal setting, and dreaming phase. You're much better taking small steps and testing than thinking about it for years before you finally launch.

A quiet start allows you to adjust, to change direction and to figure out what you're doing without feeling like you have to be perfect or successful right away without too much of a lost investment. It will help you build a strong foundation. You want to be able to learn, set up systems and really tighten up what you are offering, understanding who your person is, and the strategies you will need to succeed. And being scrappy from day one is a great mindset to have.

There is no need to have a website and all social platforms looking professional at the beginning, you don't even need a logo to start. A business is not defined by having marketing materials but having a product or service out there in the world for which you receive compensation. Note that I did not say money!

For many service providers, your first clients may not pay you, but rather work with you in order for you to get practice and in exchange, they leave you a review. This can even be a requirement for some industries such as massage therapy and organizing services. If you are not able to accept money in exchange for services as you are starting, be sure to barter for reviews and put that in writing before you begin. You may be giving away your first products and services simply to get feedback. It's more important for you to get your services and products in alignment with what your people want than to have a fancy logo and website. Knowing your person, solving their problem, and understanding where to find them are the essentials to a strong beginning.

Restaurants have soft openings and they often open to

"friends and family" for a week, then collect feedback, tweak, and then open to the public. The timeline is often quicker than what you will do due to the massive overhead for a restaurant and small profit margins but think of your own business having a soft opening.

Take one step after another until you are fully open, branded, and launched. And then you can still change things. That's the beauty of tiny! You have the flexibility to change and adapt as needed.

"Perfect is the enemy of good, shipped is better than perfect."
—Seth Godin

Starting While Working

Ideally, you can start your business while working (or as I have done while transiting out of one business to the next). For parents who are transitioning from full-time child-raising to starting a business, if you have a job or have kids who you are used to caring for them 24/7, you will have less time than say someone who lives alone and has left a job. What do you do if you are trying to fit in starting a business in a limited amount of time each day?

I have seen incredible businesses start while the owner lives what looks like a crammed, stuffed, and overflowing life. For some people, the more they have going on, the more they can get done. Why? Because they already understand the importance of every second of the day, of prioritizing and of not wasting time. There is a proverb coined by the twentieth-century British historian, Cyril Northcote Parkinson, and it's known as Parkinson's Law: "Work expands so as to fill the time available for its completion."[19]

Anyone who has ever had a block of open time and decided to see what's going on with social media knows what I mean by this. You look up and half an hour has passed and you have accomplished nothing. If you are trying to squeeze in a few hours each day of getting your new business going, it can happen, but you will need to be strategic. You will also need to have some discipline in place or two weeks will go by and you'll have not done one thing.

To start, look at your schedule. Where are the blocks of your time where nothing is scheduled? What are you doing at that time? Can you eliminate something? Maybe you don't need 2 hours each night for Netflix and chill? This is a great exercise not only for starting a new business but if you wanted to add a new revenue stream or even take up a hobby.

Time is finite. We cannot make more of it. But we can rearrange it and be more diligent about how we spend it. In

---

19 A fascinating article about Parkinson's Law and it's origin: https://www.bbc.com/worklife/article/20191107-the-law-that-explains-why-you-cant-get-anything-done

looking at what our schedules are like, we can normally start to see patterns of where there are blocks of wasted or usable time. I know of many moms who used nap times and the time between a young child going to bed and their own bedtime to fit in work. And many of us, with children or not, love those quiet early mornings before the house wakes up. But to take time, you often have to let something go and it should not be sleep.

Things to remove: Let's start with the biggest for many of us, scrolling on social media. If you look at your phone data of your social media usage each week, it can be shocking how much time is wasted here. While reading this, my editor Mallory shared that she leaves her phone out of the room while working and actually deletes apps when she notices that she is getting sucked into them too often. Both are great tips and ways to remove the temptation instead of relying on self-control. I use blockers on my phone and my computer that physically prevent me from visiting social media, and email while working. The struggle is real.

TV can be a huge place to take back time from, it may be a great way to gain an entire hour or more per day. Commute time is sometimes a big one, although the pandemic altered that for many. If you are not already, can you adjust to being remote a few days a week and gain 30 minutes each way from your commute? What are you doing in the late hours of the evenings? Are you just sitting around watching TV and snacking? Adjusting to let some of that time go, which will allow for an earlier bedtime, resulting in an extra hour or two in the morning can have incredible results from those uninterrupted 7-14 hours a week!

I have done this exercise both with wanting to read more and with wanting to write. For reading, I stopped all TV which freed up time to rearrange my schedule a bit. I don't read during the hours I used to watch TV. It was not a direct time swap, but rather, I moved other activities into that time I used to watch TV and created blocks at different times.

With writing, I created the time to write before I started writing. I had been getting up two hours earlier than usual every Wednesday for a weekly meeting. I realized that a pretty simple way to create time to write and when I write best, was to shift my wake-up every day to 5. This meant I had to shift my evening as well, to make sure I was asleep by 10 p.m. or I wouldn't function well. I found out quickly that there were two hours of the evening where I wasn't doing much. I was puttering around the house, working on a puzzle for longer than resulted in the desired unwinding time. I was willing to give up some of that evening time and give it to my mornings.

I started by moving my wake-up time earlier by 15 minutes a day. I trained my brain to do this without an alarm so I would feel rested. This sounds insane. I get that. I am a lifelong night owl and am rolling my eyes at myself right now. But I read up on this and researched how people handle getting up early to write and it was oddly easier than I thought it would be. Although I got up earlier, I was getting enough sleep. The earlier bedtime is a big part of it, and because I really wanted this to work. My husband Adam has always said that if he tells himself at night what time to wake up, it happens. One day I thought, if he can do it, I can. I tried it and it really works! Occasionally, I will sleep an extra 30 minutes, but for the most part, I wake up like a light shined in my eyes between 5 and 5:30 a.m.. On the day I must be up at 5 a.m,, I set an alarm as back up, but I woke up 5 minutes before it for two months and eventually stopped setting it. I haven't slept past 5 yet on Wednesdays, it's interesting that our brains can work like that!

I have found that it's easier if I consistently keep this schedule, so I wake up early every day. Before I was writing, I started doing other highly creative work in that time (things like rebuilding my website, which I am constantly doing) as I was training my brain to do this type of work at this time and establishing the habit. I also have been journaling first thing in the morning for years, so I was really priming myself for writing first thing. When the day came to start, I was so used to already being at my desk working at 6:15 a.m. that writing until 7:45 a.m. felt natural and I was hitting my word goal from the start.

I went into such detail on this so you can see how having a strategy can help so much in the success of creating time. There have been countless scenarios in my past when I have not had luck making time and almost all those times were lacking in having a strategy and a plan that broke down what I had to do into tiny steps. I know that I am an all-or-nothing person, so if I am not putting myself on a plan of daily small actions, it will have a much greater chance of not working. You may be the opposite, and that's fine! My point is to find the strategies which work for you.

Know yourself, look at the data of your schedule and how you spend your time, create a strategic plan that makes it easy to succeed and go for it. You'll be amazed at what you can get done in just 90 minutes a day if you plan your priorities and stay consistent with your efforts. You will also have the excitement for the new project of your business on your side and will make great progress if you have discipline, focus, and consistency. The first few months are always the most thrilling, use the energy naturally occurring at that time to set your habits.

Starting With an Open Schedule

Besides having a strategy and a plan, I recommend you put yourself on a schedule. Ironically, having a wide-open schedule is often a much bigger problem for people when it comes to starting a business. Why? Because there isn't much going on in the first few months that you *have* to do. Sure, you would like to get the ball going quickly, but if there are no clients or deadlines being held accountable by another person, you can quickly fall into the trap of doing nothing and calling it work.

You can also end up having Netflix marathons or being on social media all day as you don't know what else to do with yourself. It will be up to you to create your own timeline, hold yourself accountable and prioritize your time. It's easy to fall into the habit of time-wasting in this case. It's also easy to start to add useless busywork to fill your days so you feel like you're doing things.

What is a solution to this mess?

Number One - Get Organized

Decide how you want to organize yourself, be it Google calendar, a paper planner, a notebook, to-do software, or a combo of them all. You may use one system for a year and switch it up. I have found that many super-productive people are constantly trying new systems and love looking for new solutions. Whatever your system is, the key is that you have to use it. Time blocking should become your friend.

Number Two - Get Accountability

Find an accountability partner. Not someone you pay, but

a friend who also has goals and wants to have to answer to someone each week. Set up a standing zoom call and check-in for 30 min to one hour each week. You can structure it however you like, but a good place to start is to each list three goals for the week and report back on them. When you outline your goals, your partner can push back if they think it sounds too vague or too big or small of a task. You also can discuss wins and celebrate your successes, especially the tiny things.

Number Three - Get Focused

Fill your time with useful tasks. If you do not have clients and customers yet, using this time to build your foundation is a fantastic idea. If you have started to have clients and customers, you can start to use the input to create your systems. Systems for admin tasks, social media, content creation, on-boarding clients, how you handle fulfillment and on-and-on. You can write them up and create your checklists for these as well, but if you have no business yet, do not guess at these. They need to be created from what you do, guessing will waste your time.

You can network. I highly stress this one. Get out there and talk to people. This is a great time to visit all the groups you find interesting and decide which you want to join. Get on committees. Give. Right now you will have the most time ever to give. Volunteer and help where you can. It will make you feel better, and you'll do good. Fun fact, volunteering 100 hours per year is the magic number. If you volunteer more then you will not increase happiness. But over 800 hours a year, it will start to decrease your happiness. If you volunteer less, it will make you less happy. Aim for two hours a week! Joining a committee or board is a great way to do this.

When you are visiting groups, you should set up a 1:1 coffee (all of these events, coffees and volunteering can absolutely be done via Zoom by the way!) with two people who you meet or who look interesting. When you have these conversations, start to establish relationships. You can also ask them which networking groups they love to add to your list of groups to visit.

When deciding which groups to join, it's important to visit many so you find the places where you want to have relationships with most of the membership. Otherwise, you'll be wasting your time and money by joining. Doing all of this leg work before you're busy with clients is a fantastic use of your time. The relationships you build foundations on now will be nurtured, of course, over the years, but if you have vast blocks of time to find your people, the ROI on that time spent will be incredible down the road.

As you get busier, you will back off from networking but don't disappear or you will undo all your work. Make sure to stay involved in your 1-3 groups and always be nurturing those relationships!

You Should Be Embarrassed by Your First Offering

If you are creating a product or service from scratch, it's easy to sit on it and tweak it and keep it to yourself and never actually launch. I do this constantly. After writing this manuscript, I had to push hard to keep going, I was all, "OMG, I wrote a book, I did it, that's my goal!" It took many reminders to myself and from my accountability partner that getting the book out is the goal, not just the fun, creative part. It's scary to be vulnerable and put yourself out there! It's also more fun for many of us to do creative work than things like editing. But there will be no business if you do not sell the thing you do. You have to take that step.

It's a common theme in the tech world to talk about the first rendition of your offering to be completely embarrassing to you years later. If it's not, you launched too late. This is also why networking is so valuable. You can put it out there, see the reactions and tweak at a faster rate than if you waited for enough customers or clients to find you.

You want to avoid the perfectionism trap at all costs. If you are wondering if your product or service is ready, ask yourself a few questions. Does it bring value and solve a problem for your person? Are you proud of what you have done and want to share it with others? Are you not launching because you are worried about succeeding, failing, having people judge you, or what people who are not your ideal person will say? If you answered yes to the first two, it's launch time!

Sum It Up:

- You will never be ready to start. Don't wait until you are ready! You also will almost always be embarrassed by that first offering later.
- Stay scrappy. Wait on the big website, expensive logo, and anything you have to hire out for until you start selling. DIY as much as you can for the first few months to year.
- Remove time wasting tasks and activities and replace them with useful ones to grow your business. You have more time than you think.

Chapter 8:

Failure Is the Goal

When was the last time you had a big failure? Failure is necessary for success. First off, you need to understand that there is a difference between the failure of doing something and not having the result that you wanted and the failure of never taking action. We're going to be talking about the type of failure from doing something and not getting the result you want from your action.

You put yourself out there, you tried, and it did not go as planned. Perhaps you have started a business in the past and it failed. You never got clients, never made money, or never got it off the ground. Perhaps you have put on a big event and nobody showed up. Perhaps you have tried to get a job and did not get it. These are all the types of failure that sting, but failures like these are necessary for success.

Strive for this type of failure because the more you go big, the more you'll fail and the better the chance that you will succeed. But you do have to fail. Because if you're not aiming big enough, putting yourself in the situations where there is the potential that you'll fail, then you're not going big enough to have great success. It goes hand-in-hand.

Why is it important to fail? The first reason is for the sake of experience. Obviously, if you're not aiming big enough to fail, you are not taking the kind of risk where you're getting the experiences where you can learn from them. You are not figuring out what your strengths and weaknesses are. If you're not taking the kind of risk that ends up in a big failure, then you're not learning what you need to do to keep going and get better at what you do.

You can get knowledge from failure. In the process of doing things beyond your comfort zone that are a reach for you to aim for, you will learn you are not right about everything. Which means you are going to have to do a good deal of research and testing. Which results in your learning about something. There are so many ways that you can learn. Including learning what not to do. Even if the outcome is not what you wanted, it's about the process.

The process is the most important thing. You need to understand that anything that you're doing, be it goal setting, be it taking chances, whatever it is, that it's all about the process. That's where the real work happens. It's where you're taking risks. It's where you're learning. It's where you're growing. These are all things that are essential to success.

Another thing that you'll get from failure is resilience. Because if you fail and then you get up and do things again, you are building resilience. You're also building your courage, your confidence, and your self-esteem. You will learn that when you fail, you will not die. This is why sports can be so wonderful to get involved in when you're a little kid (and as an adult). Through sports, you learn that you will both win and lose. You learn that yes, failure will happen, but you get back up and keep going and going and going and going and going and then do it all again the next time. You learn that even if you fail most times, that the one time where you hit success, that's what makes it all worth it.

The other day a friend mentioned that it doesn't seem like much keeps me down. I asked why she said that, and she referred to a recent failure I experienced. My reply was that I fail all the time and that this was a small one so why would I even be down? I hardly paused with this one, I just kept going. This made me think about the big failures in my life. Those milestone moments. I have been fired. I have quit. I have been in situations where I cried continuously because of how bad things were. I've gotten myself involved in projects where I didn't even know why I said 'yes' to begin with. On a personal level, I have failed spectacularly as well. Yet here I am, still going on having mostly forgotten about all those failures, but being all the wiser for them.

Failure helps you grow. If you are taking chances and learning new things and doing the things and taking the risks and all of that, you are, without realizing it, immensely helping yourself grow. Let's for a second, reflect on the wisdom of the wonderful Brene Brown. When you find yourself doing something that you've already experienced, the universe dares you to evolve. We are learning from our failures in so many ways, including that action of picking ourselves back up and the action of learning from our mistakes. This is all growth. This is all maturity and great reasons why failure is key.

This brings us to the value of failure, the learned, the biggest lessons, the opportunity to have that growth, the things that you're doing to forge greatness. We hear this in all the tech success stories. None of the founders would have the growth or the level of success they achieved if they had not picked themselves back up off the ground after repeatedly failing miserably. Tech is one of the best ways of really showing the importance of failure in success because with technology, it doesn't work until it works.

I have some engineering background, and I did not pursue a career in coding because when you are coding, there's often something as simple as a misplaced character that stops everything from working. For those of us who are prone to typos, this can be a nightmare. If there is one teensy typo in there everything will fail and you have to comb through the code to find that one misplaced character to fix it. You can write the best code in the world, but if it does not run correctly and the results do not happen from it, then it is a failure. But no one just walks away at that point, they simply look for the error. And then for the error after that, until it's fixed and working.

It's really one of the fields where perseverance is built right into the practice of it because it won't run if you fail, and you just keep pushing and pushing and pushing until it works. Then you tweak it and tweak it and tweak it until it works better. We've all heard the stories of how two geeks started building something in their garage and they just kept going and going and going and going until they got it right. The real reason why they experienced massive success is that failure wasn't even a blip on their radar. They just kept plowing through until it worked.

The final reason why failure is great is that it makes you think about paying it forward. And that is a wonderful part of failure. When you realize there are people who will be there to help pick you up after you fail. And that there are people who will give you a new opportunity in the face of failure. And that is a wonderful reminder that you too can be that person for somebody who you see fail.

It's so essential for successful businesses that we all

work together. Even when you are both in the same field or competitors, there's still so much that you can do to help each other. With the whole pay-it-forward concept, it's not just about looking for people in distress. It's about having community and having a group where every time you're failing, you have people there who have your back and support you.

I'm a big fan of community. I love nothing more than a group of people who are supportive of each other. This makes it so you feel that you can fail because you have your crew behind you cheering you on, understanding what you're going through. And sometimes to take the risks, you need a little bit of that.

Recovering From Failure

Now let's talk about recovering from failure. That community and group that I just went into, may be the most essential aspect of recovering, especially if you are in a specific field. This could be anything from being part of an organization or an association; a mastermind, a networking group, or just a group of friends that you talk about work and life. I'll give a shameless plug for the Doers Shakers Makers Facebook group[20] as it's a wonderful community accessible to anyone with a Facebook account and you are all welcome to join us. But really, any group where you can feel comfortable enough to open up and talk freely about things like experiencing failure is the right group. It's essential

20 Come on over: https://www.facebook.com/groups/doersshakersmakers

if you're going to start to think big and try a lot of things that you have people in your corner that you feel like you can put yourself out there a little bit more.

Let's say you have a failure. We'll use an example of having a failed podcast, as my first podcast failed. The first thing you need to do to recover is to ignore the haters. My podcast following was not large and thankfully I didn't have haters yelling at me, but sometimes you may have haters happen. You just ignore those haters. You pay no attention to them. Do not read your reviews. Do not google yourself to see what people are saying. Absolutely do not engage with them. If you fail at something, you just pick yourself up and move on.

Remember that it is okay to fail. That's a big part of moving on. It's the mindset. It is letting yourself know, especially women, that it's ok to have attempted something and to not have been perfect with it. We've been programmed to think perfection is the goal. Perfection is not the goal; the process is the goal. You need to work on getting over that trap of perfectionism and start to understand it doesn't matter what the result is. It matters that you tried and that is a big part of recovering from failure.

Having tried shows how important it is for you to mentally accept failure. You can't start a business and the first time you have a failure you quit. You should be constantly throwing things against the wall in your business at the beginning to see what sticks. Do you know what that means? That means trying things and failing. I want you to be comfortable with going out there and failing a lot. You need to have all the traits that we've already talked about. The experience, the knowledge, the resilience, the growth, knowing to pay it forward, and a community. You need to have all of that in place if you're going to succeed and own a business because it is hard, long work. You need to have the ability to bounce back. That may be the most important thing for business success.

The next thing is to use failure as leverage, so let's say in the example of the failed podcast. My first podcast failed and within a month, I had a new podcast. You can't say, "Oh, I failed. I can never do anything again." No, I really was and am to this day so incredibly grateful because that first podcast taught me all the technical stuff I needed to know about podcasting. It was a different format. It was a different subject matter. All of that was quite different, but it taught me the basics of how to record, how to upload, and how to create and build the back end on my own and integrate it into my website. All those things were learned by doing that first podcast. Leverage whatever your failure was and use that for your next success.

Failure also provides a great opportunity to review your goals. Sometimes failure happens because we drift away from our own mission in the excitement over a new and fun-sounding opportunity. Even though we know, deep down inside, that it's not a good fit, we still get excited. I am no stranger to this happening. A great example of this is what happened with my jewelry brand. There was a collection of jewelry that was a massive, very expensive two year-long failure that involved a lot of people, a lot of photoshoots, and a lot of products. So much money was involved, and it was a colossal failure from the beginning. I should have looked at my mission and looked at my goals and I realized that it did not line up with either my mission or vision. I knew it deep down, but I was so excited about the newness that I plowed ahead. I don't regret it, as I learned a great deal and made wonderful connections from it. It also made me review my goals and reassess what my mission and vision were as I had been slacking on revisiting them.

Having that one big top goal that you know that you can benchmark everything that you're doing against can be incredibly helpful for this reason. This is why that's so essential to spend some time setting quarterly, monthly, and weekly goals. When you fail, revisiting your goals is a great way to pick yourself up and have that "Oh, this is why that didn't work" or "What did I learn and what can I do differently next time?" conversation with yourself.

The last thing about recovering is creating a massive action plan. You don't just say, "I failed and now life is over and I'm going to roll up in a ball and stay that way for the rest of time." I'll be nice, I'll give you one day. When I shut down my business after almost 16 years, I gave myself four days. I thought that due to how big of a thing this was, I should wallow, process, feel for a few days longer than necessary. I took one day, I tried to take the four days, but I was already chomping at the bit to work on the next thing. You too will do the next thing for you, whatever that is.

Admittedly, I have been through a lot of failures, so I'm resilient. Not everybody is like I am, we all process differently. But try to get your wallowing out of your system quickly. Give it its space and then get back up and put a massive action plan in place. What is your next thing? This can be as simple as, what are you doing today? Do something. It does not have to be work-related, but just something that gets you in action and it will make a huge difference in getting your mental state back in place. I like to organize things in my house. That's just my happy place. It gives me a little bit of instant gratification. It helps me get back on that horse. I have a little win and it gives enough confidence to boost to get back at it.

Go ahead and fail. Failure is great. I want you all to fail. If you're not failing, you're not going big enough!

Sum It Up:

- You cannot achieve great success without failure, you might as well get comfortable with it. Failure is a necessary part of success. It means you are pushing yourself to the levels you need to reach to succeed.
- There are so many incredible lessons to learn from failure, from resilience to learning new skills.
- Having a support system in place will help you recover from failure and see it as a part of success, not the end of it.

PART II:

Building The Framework
of Your Business

Chapter 9:

Am I Doing This Right? The Logistics of Starting Your Business.

A common question I get from new clients is: "Am I doing this right?" Rarely do talented people think they did things correctly in setting up their businesses. Even if they at one point were confident that they took the correct steps, they'll talk to a fellow business owner who did things differently and start to completely doubt the steps they took.

You may have gathered by this point that there is not an exact science to starting a business. This largely is due to there being multiple options with each step, which in turn makes it so the outcomes are infinite. This is exactly why I tell tiny business owners all the time to not trust formulas for success. It's incredibly hard to replicate the exact results that another business has had or even what your own business did last year and getting the same results. Owning a business is about constantly iterating, testing, tweaking, and then repeating this process over and over again. As long as you are starting a business the right way for *you*, then you can feel confident that it's the "right" way.

That being said as far as starting a legal entity goes, there are laws around owning a business. And there are also a few things required that are the standard practices in the U.S. You will need to do an Internet search to see what your state and county laws are[21], and most likely it will include many, if not all of the things, we'll discuss in this chapter. As with everything, I suggest that you start small and expand as you grow.

The reminder I will keep stressing throughout is that a vast number of businesses fail largely due to lack of cash flow. Don't spend money on what you hope to grow to be, spend money on what you need now. You really can change just about anything around later, as long as you have been legally operating correctly and paying the IRS along the way. And you can fix that too, it will just cost more at once.

What is the most important thing to be doing legally from the start? Paying taxes and registering with the local government. The least important? Worrying about the formation. You do however have to have a name with any formation, so we'll begin there.

What's In A Name?

The hardest decision for many pre-business owners to make is

21 Search "*your state* laws about starting a business" and you should get the results you need.

what to name the business. Much of this has to do with what is also available as far as domains and social media handles go, so once you start brainstorming, be prepared to domain search and rule out anything that is not available with the exact name .com. You want people to be able to find you quickly and easily and using anything besides .com can make that tricky.

A few tips. Don't use your name as your business name. If you are in the knowledge business, you may need to, and in this case, still have a business name. A personal example is that when I officially became a jewelry designer, my late stepfather, who had been a corporate lawyer in NY, said, I know everyone is going to give you advice, and you can ignore everything except this: "You do not want your name tied forever to the business." Why? Well, lawsuits to start. Obviously, if something goes wrong, you as a person are a bit more protected. But mainly because if you reach a point where you do want to sell, you can lose the rights to design or work in that area under your name.

This scenario is exemplified by Kate Spade and her story as a handbag designer. She partnered with Neiman Marcus about four years into the business and within 10 years, sold to them outright. That sentence should be read again, she only owned the handbag business for 13 or so years! It was sold long before most people knew about her bags at all. After selling, she changed her last name to Valentine (she used one of her many middle names, which had been her grandmother's last name) to separate herself from the brand. She created an accessories brand shortly before her death, Frances Valentine (her daughter's name.) that continued.[22]

As Kate Spade became a household name, it must have been confusing and I'm sure was complicated for her to deal with on a personal and professional level. There are many difficult things you may not be able to avoid in business, but this you can avoid by simply using anything besides your own name.

Also, beware of using a name that defines what you do. It makes a pivot hard to do if you change direction. Why box yourself in when you never know what will happen? My jewelry company was a mix of website design, fine art, and jewelry when I started it. That was the thing back then for makers. And the name worked well for all the things I was working on and although I often would get a weird look over having a name like Manic Trout for jewelry. The Indie magazines loved it, but sometimes I got weird comments in blog write-ups. Often though editors told me it was a great name and they never forgot it, an editor at Teen Vogue said everyone who dealt with the jewelry loved the name. So, there's that for having a unique

---

22 Few people know the entire timeline of Kate Spade, I was lucky to hear her speak in the early days of her brand and was always fascinated with her brand. You can read a great summary here: https://www.glamour.com/story/kate-spade-life-career-timeline

name, memorability.

A great reason to right off the bat to have a business name besides your own is that it will make switching to a different business formation later easier. You want to start small and grow as you go, but it's smart to think ahead and make that growth have as few bumps in the road as possible.

As you grow, you can always create an umbrella with a new business name. If you choose a name that has what you do in it, down the road, you can create a business name and form an LLC with it and can then have multiple DBAs under it, including that first one. The easiest way to describe how this works is that Dax Shepard has done this with his podcast Armchair Expert. That is the umbrella company, and he now has a variety of podcasts that have their own names, yet still exist under Armchair Expert.

A word on made-up names. Do it. Xerox for example is a completely made-up name! Most big brands choose single words, but they are becoming harder to buy the URLs for, so there is the tech trick of replacing letters like S with X. Keep in mind that the goal is to make it simple and easy to find. Doers Shakers Makers, which had little thought, is never said right. And it's three words. It's a horrible name as everyone is confused with the order.

Partners

Before we get to formations. I want to talk about having a business partner. I strongly urge you not to have a business partner. The percentage of business partnerships that go well is low. It should not be taken lightly as you will be legally and monetarily bound to that person. You need to take the idea of forming this relationship more seriously than marriage as it can be more difficult to get out of than a marriage.

You should have conversations about values, expectations, definitions of success, work style, how much you each expect to work, and go through everything we have discussed up to this point with a potential partner to ensure you are on the same page. You should have in writing, what you are each bringing to the partnership financially and what you expect from each other. You should discuss what will happen if one wants to leave the business. Will they have to be bought out? Will the business close? Also, how will you each be paid and how much, as the business begins to profit? These are all incredibly important conversations.

You will not be able to form a DBA and must form a Partnership, LLC or Corp. Be sure and research how you will be protected in a partnership in your state and county before you sign anything. Business partnerships are a big deal, do not go into one flippantly.

If you are forming a partnership in order to get funding where they provide equity and you provide the "sweat equity", AKA doing the actual work, consider all other options for funding. If you are forming a partnership because you're nervous, lack confidence in yourself, or want to have a friend holding your hand through the process, those are not reasons to have a partnership. Very few partnerships succeed, 50% - 80% of them fail simply due to the partnership, not the business.[23]

Business Formations

Business formations are possibly the most controversial step in starting a business. Everyone thinks they are right on this and their way is the best. Let me clear this all up for you. Whatever you want to do is fine, and having a DBA is an excellent place to start. You can easily change it later, and you may never need to, depending on your business. Anyone who says that a DBA is not a real business is being a judgmental jerk.

Most banks will require that you have at least a DBA filed in order to open a business checking account. You also will need a DBA filed to collect sales tax in my state of Texas and my previous state of NY, your state may differ. How you form your business will determine which income tax you have to file. A good rule of thumb is the more money your business makes, the

23 Why partnerships fail: https://www.inc.com/marissa-levin/the-5-most-important-strategies-for-creating-a-successful-business-partnership.html

more structure you'll want in the formation.

There is nothing wrong with being a DBA as you begin and grow. Focus on staying in business for that first year and making a profit. Once you get out of the hobby level you can change your formation. You should prove it can even get out of hobby level (there is a list on the IRS website[24], but a good rule of thumb is $12k or less in a year in sales with a profit) before you even think about declaring you're a corporation (if ever). A DBA will however not protect your name beyond your county. This is fine while you are starting, but once you become more known you'll want to change your formation. This is typically something that will become an issue a few years in, not year one.

Interestingly, when you look up information on formations, the articles that really push LLCs and S Corps are often on websites for companies that profit from helping you form one of these entities. One of the reasons they write compelling articles about why you must have a formation beyond a DBA is that they get paid to form them. They often use scare tactics to encourage fear-based decisions. Be aware of who you are listening to and always look into what they gain from your decision.

That's solid advice for everything you encounter in business… what's in it for the person telling you? If nothing, if they are friends or family who own businesses, mentors, companies like

24 Hobby or a business: https://www.irs.gov/newsroom/hobby-or-business-irs-offers-tips-to-decide

SCORE, people like me, you're probably good. But if they will be paid based on the outcome, keep that in mind.

Options for Formations

As the point of formations is to determine how you structure your taxes, we are going directly to the Internal Revenue Service website to explain the differences between formations.[25]

Sole Proprietorship/DBA: You own the unincorporated business by yourself. You file a 1040 and Schedule C. For Sole proprietorship, you are using your own name to do business, not a name with your name in it, simply your name. If you are using a name other than your own (which I do recommend), you need to file a DBA that stands for Doing Business As. Your DBA is registered with the County. This means that your name can be registered by anyone who is not in your county. This is not much of a problem if you own your URL and social handle, but can be problematic as you grow, especially if you make or manufacture products. The filing fee at the County Clerk's office is under $50 and the process is fast and easy.

Partnerships: Similar to a DBA, you need to register your name with the County Clerk's office. Your taxes are reported on your individual tax returns. The partnership must file a partnership information return with the IRS each year.

---

25 Visit www.IRS.gov for more information on formations.

LLC: Limited Liability Company is allowed by state statute, and not all states allow it. It's a hybrid model between a corporation and a partnership. Depending on your state, the regulations vary, so be sure to check with your state on the specifics. The owners of an LLC are called members and you can have as many owners as you want. It offers more protection to your individual assets than a DBA. Depending on your state, it costs $50 to $500 to form before fees. Filing for your EIN number can cost $0 to $200. LLCs filed as partnerships file the partnership return and LLCs taxed as corporations file either the C-Corp or S-Corp tax return.

Corporations: The most formal and expensive to form. A corporation is a legal entity for conducting business. It is a separate entity from those who founded it and accepts the responsibilities of the organization. It is taxed and held legally liable like a person would be. The main reason people are drawn to it is the idea that they are protected legally. However, keep in mind that while that seems great and the cost to incorporate is a $500 filing fee (you file in Delaware, research that) and $0-$200 to file for your EIN number. So far, like an LLC, no big deal. But, the annual costs to own a corporation can be crazy.

You will pay an annual state fee of $145 (to Delaware, yes, I think this is weird too) and taxes to every state you do business in. Not an issue until the past few years where states are wanting taxes paid for online transactions. You will pay the start fee for the state you live in and if you have team members or contract employees in another state. Having a VA in California could end up with you paying another state fee, $400 in the case of CA. Then you have the mountain of tax filing per year for a corporation. You'll have to pay $1000-$5000 per year for accounting and filing because if you do it yourself and mess it up, the fines for incorrect filing can start at $10,000.[26]

In an S Corp, profits and losses flow through the owners. In a C Corp, the corporation retains its profits and losses but has double taxation earnings and shareholders are taxed on dividends. Both C and S corps file corporate tax returns, file an annual report in their incorporating state, conduct annual meetings, and must meet federal and state record-keeping obligations. To finish off with a slap, if you fail and have to close your business, it will be $1000 to $2000 to close the corporation. Start small, not with a corporation. Get through your first year. Proceed from there.

Sales Tax

What is taxed is determined by the state and county. Most states who collect sales tax will require sales tax to be collected on physical products. Some states require that it's collected on

26 How much it costs to get a Corp up and running: https://slidebean.com/blog/startups-us-corporation-costs

potentially physical products, such as PDFs. Some states require taxes collected on all services, some on specific services. Please research your state's requirements as they are subject to change with new laws.

There are new laws being proposed and passed about collecting sales tax for states you do not live in but sell to online. This too is ever-changing. Selling through sites like Etsy and Amazon allows you to grant them permission to collect and pay the sales to specific states on your behalf. On your own e-commerce site, there are plugins you can often add to help you figure these out as well. As you grow and in future years, having a bookkeeper and/or CPA can help immensely in this area. In the first year or so, you can usually manage it well on your own. Remember though, that even if you pay someone to file your taxes, you are still responsible for incorrect filing, it is you who would be fined and in extreme cases, jailed. It is important that you understand your taxes and what you are paying.

In your own state, you need to register your business with the Comptroller if you sell taxable products and services. You will receive a stamped and sealed document that you must display if you have a brick n' mortar location. If you are selling products in person, you must have your sales tax permit with you when you are selling. This applies to shows, markets, food trucks, any place where you are selling your goods. It is common practice for police to attend events and ask all vendors to show them this document.

Most states have a base sales tax[27] amount to be charged, and specific counties will charge different rates. Many people opt to charge a flat sales tax rate for their state, but if you are doing shows, when you pay your tax bill online on the comptroller site, you will have to specify what counties you sold in if you were in person. It sounds complicated, but once you set it up and get going, it's simple. Your tax schedule will be either monthly, quarterly, or annually depending on the amount you collect.

Again, you can outsource this to a bookkeeper, but it is essential that you understand your finances and what is coming in and out as you will be held liable if there is a problem. The first year or two, while you are growing, is a wonderful opportunity to learn and understand this area while it's less overwhelming.

Permits, Insurance, Trademark, NDA's

There are certain businesses that will require permits and insurance[28]. Be sure to research the type of business you are starting to know if you have all the correct paperwork filed.

Anything with food will require specific permits.[29] You may

27 A list of all sales tax rates in the U.S. can be found here: https://www.salestaxinstitute.com/resources/rates

28 The SBA overview of common business insurance needs: https://www.sba.gov/business-guide/launch-your-business/get-business-insurance

29 FDA requirements for a food business: https://www.fda.gov/food/food-indus-

need zoning permits, health permits, occupational permits and of course sales tax.

If you have anyone on the premise, have a brick n' mortar business, or do shows, you will need to have liability insurance, usually a 1 to 2 million dollar policy. Look into your homeowner's policy about riders. When you do large shows, like tradeshows, it is required to show proof of insurance, sometimes with your application.

Trademarks

Intellectual property law is a vast subject.[30] I will simply say that if you are tiny, until you prove your business is viable and start gaining traction, don't worry about trademarking your brand. Have the URL and all the social sites, but a trademark is not necessary if no one knows who you are yet. Understand that having a trademark also means that you are the one who will need to enforce with legal representation anyone violating that trademark. Often trademarking leads to spending all your time chasing down violations and all of your money in the process. Tread carefully with trademarks and do not listen solely to the person who would financially benefit from this scenario, aka a lawyer who you would pay to chase down violations.

---

try/how-start-food-business

30 A great overview of intellectual property law: https://www.chamberofcommerce.org/intellectual-property-for-small-businesses/

If you are seeing clients, you should have a simple NDA (Non-Disclosure Agreement)[31] ready as a pdf that you both sign prior to working together. You can send it via email and keep it on record for both of your protection. You are stating that neither of you will talk about each other's business or knowledge without consent. You can often find these for free online and customize them for your business.

As you grow, the need for more protection may come up, stay scrappy when you can, but make sure you are operating legally and protecting yourself! If you are looking to where you can cut costs, keep it to what you need *now*. Why pay for protection for shows for two years if you are not doing shows? That $1000 could be much more useful elsewhere and can set up in minutes when you need it.

As soon as you are occupying that space, selling taxable items, or doing business, be sure you have those protections in place. And always think about who is giving you the advice to spend money on formations and big financial and legal decisions. CPAs and lawyers are in business as well, and they need to sell their services. Eager and unaware tiny business owners are often targets for unneeded, high price tag services that are not necessary.

---

31 More info on NDA's: https://legaldictionary.net/non-disclosure-agreement/

Business Formation To-Do's:

1. Decide on business structure and what options you have in your state (sole proprietorship/DBA, LLC, corporation).
2. Being a sole proprietor is a great place to start and you can always change later. You need to file a DBA if you are using a name besides your own. The easiest way is to go to your County Clerks office.
3. Open a bank account with your DBA and be able to have business accounts for Paypal, Stripe, et all to be deposited to.
4. If you are collecting sales tax (selling goods and certain services), register with your state's Comptroller.
5. As a sole proprietor/DBA, you will be able to use your personal social security number as your EIN (employer identification number) for tax purposes. For other formations, you need to apply for an EIN.
6. If you have a DBA, you will file your taxes annually with a 1040 Schedule C. (using Turbo Tax will be fine to start). With other formations, research the protocol in your state.
7. To be safe, you may want to set aside 25%-30% of all earned income for taxes.

8. Having a simple spreadsheet in Google sheets or Excel for your sales with the date, type of service or products bought, customer info, hours, and how they paid and rate will be immensely helpful as you grow.
9. If you add another sheet with expenses it can be super helpful at the end of the year.
10. Set up a free CRM or create a spreadsheet to start tracking clients

Sum It Up:

- There is not a one size fits all formula for business success, no matter what that Instagram marketer is telling you. Understanding the options and making a rational decision for your business needs (not based on what people are profiting off of) is an excellent way to begin.
- Partnerships succeed only 30% of the time. Proceed with caution.
- Begin small and grow as you go. This is true for most things in your business, including your formation.

Chapter 10:

Forget Business Plans

Do you need a business plan? No. I really wanted to leave it at that, but you deserve more. I will also amend my answer to say, not unless you need to borrow money. But as you may have noticed, I am pushing you to stay as scrappy as possible, to only get funding if you need a physical location and have no other options. To get money at all, you will need a business plan. You can find your local SCORE[32] chapter for guidance there.

Great, now we have covered what you don't need. What you do need, is to make sure that you do research in what you are looking to start a business in, to understand who your competitors are, to know who your person is and then to create a simple marketing plan, a launch schedule, and your goals for the first quarter. More likely than not, much will change for you in the first year. You may end up having a completely different business than you planned on, depending on how you enjoy the work, and the problems you want to solve. So often, the

32 Find your local SCORE chapter: https://www.score.org/

business plans created before you begin are abandoned as you start to test things in real life.

You also are probably completely overwhelmed by the thought of creating a business plan and it's stopping you from moving forward and taking action. The thought of a business plan can make many people stuck. Then what steps do you take first? The first thing you should do is a bit of research, and then get out there and talk to people. Explain what you are trying to do and start doing it. You can plan more in-depth once you know people will pay you to do what you want to do. You can change your prices, you can offer different services or products, you can change your business name, you can do anything you want. Isn't that why you started this whole thing? For the freedom and flexibility that comes with it? Don't tie yourself up in a rigid plan that you guessed before you even started.

What Money Will You Need to Start?

When it comes down to figuring out how much money you'll need to start a business, well, that of course, depends. There is no rule for this. For many people leaving Corporate America to start their own business, it's often suggested to have a year of expenses in your personal account. Well for that matter, most from that background will also advise gathering all the seed money you can. And to never use credit cards or personal money to fund a business.

However, I have yet to meet someone who is starting a tiny business based on their talents who is flush with cash. I would even say that those who start making money the fastest are not typically in that latter category. Being a bit hungry can be a great motivator and many of those who need to start a business right now are perhaps in a position of some savings but no one to turn to for investment money. If they are lucky, they may have a spouse, partner, or parents who can guarantee they will not starve. But let it be said, loudly, that there is no shame in working full time while you get going and part-time until it's a reliable income.

Start as small as possible and stay scrappy. Keep your overhead as low as possible. Use the free versions of software for as long as you can. Get a library card and embrace the DIY culture. There is a vast amount of free information out there to help you get going. Use it.

When do you need to think about funding? If you are wanting to start a business that involves having something manufactured, when you need a brick n' mortar location, when you need a large vehicle, like a food truck, a large amount of inventory, a restaurant, these types of things. Not fancy offices with foosball tables or 20 employees to do nothing but make your ego feel stroked. But if you require something large and you don't have the capital, that is when you look into funding.

If however, you are providing a service, are drop shipping products, or are doing something that's around just you solving a problem for clients, then stop looking for monetary handouts, and if needed, add an additional income such as consulting, freelance work, retail, hospitality, or temp work. There is no shame in that game. Then focus on selling your products or services and start that cash coming in.

The old way to start a business was to create a business plan based on market research and projections (aka guesses), spend months creating your perfect product or service, having a fancy logo designed and a website built for you and then introducing yourself to the world. Thanks to tech and innovation, we've now realized that is not the smart plan.

Now we take our idea, we create a prototype, and we test. What does test mean? We sell it, or give it away, we receive feedback, we tweak it and repeat this process. We do this until we have a profitable product or service and then we add on revenue streams based on what the needs are of our clients and customers.

This means that first, we have cash coming in from the start, second, we are getting a real-time and accurate understanding of the market, and third that we are keeping a low overhead.

Don't Quit Your Day Job

When can you quit your job? When you are steadily earning enough to pay your bills and still invest in the business. Some will say that if you believe in yourself and take the leap, the money will follow. I say that worrying about how you are going to eat and where you will live will add such an extreme level of stress that you will make horrible business decisions and set yourself up to fail. If you have an income when you start, don't shut it off to give yourself "the pressure" to succeed. Use goal-setting, deadlines, and an accountability partner to do that and keep a roof over your head.

Two years after I (kind of) started a side business and four years after I got married (the first time), life came to a screeching halt. I realized I did not want to have kids and my ex-husband realized that he did not want to be married to an entrepreneur. That was that. I found an apartment that could fit me, my dog, my easel, and jewelry supplies and I poured myself into creating anytime I wasn't working. I realized that jewelry seemed to be the obvious path to follow before Etsy and social media. There was little information out there about how to get a business off the ground as a jewelry designer and maker.

I built a snazzy website with a shopping cart and off I went. A year or so into the business, Etsy began and with it, the resurgence of the handmade maker movement. I was a little younger than the names that made it big, but I still was caught on the wave of that time and started attracting press. Being just outside of Manhattan, this also caught the eyes of a publicist and I started paying her more each year than I had made the first year I was out of college. No problem though, business was booming and with my still full-time job, I was rolling right along.

I quit the job I had taken after I got divorced to make sure I could cover rent and food while pouring everything I made back into the business. That's when I learned a few things about myself. The first was that if I am not forced to stop working (it was for another job, but whatever), I will not stop. I will not talk to people; I will do nothing but put my head down and keep going. This did not do great things for my mental state. As a big surprise, talking to people is good for you. The second was that in business if you get super busy from a piece of press and forget to work on future business, you will not have much future business. The stress of that financially combined with my not talking to people was not great emotionally.

I started looking around to see what was out there in alignment with the only jobs I had had so far that earned enough money to make having a side job worth it, which was managing bars. It would leave my days open to work and provide benefits. I made a few calls and immediately got an offer I couldn't refuse, a private club in my town was looking for a new General Manager. The club was only open Fri-Sun. I would have (almost) all week to work on my business, it was perfect. Now, mind you, over the weekend and the two afternoons a week I had to go into the office there, I typically worked 40-60 hours, but whatever, I didn't talk to people outside of work anyway.

Taking the financial pressure off having to support me AND my business ended up being the best thing I ever did. Perhaps I had gone full time too early, perhaps it was just a bad stroke of luck, but I learned a good deal from the experience. The press started pouring in after that, including Women's Wear Daily, all of the big fashion magazines and the Real Simple holiday gift guide. That gift guide in the winter of 2008, right as the recession began, was insane. They told me to have 2,000 pairs of the featured earrings ready. I sold over 10,000 pairs of earrings in six weeks. I employed my entire club staff in my studio during the week and did not sleep. I cried a lot. I worked harder than I ever had in my life. The ding from email orders was so constant that it sounded like an arcade in the studio. It was crazy. It was amazing. I learned more from that than from years of being employed and running other people's businesses. I also opted to not quit my job and enjoy the cushion and chaos of two full-time jobs. I stayed doing both until I made the decision three years later to move to Austin, TX.

Biggest lessons learned? There is no magic time to go full time. You can't predict when a wave of businesses will happen and so much of it is luck. One wave does not mean you are set going forward. If I had not gone back to work full time would things have corrected and smoothed out? Maybe? But it was what I needed at the time. Understand that it's ok to change your mind, to get a side job, to not be a blazing, overnight success. That you are not a bad person, or a failure if you realize you are not making enough money or getting all that you need from your business full time. Reality check: most businesses touted by the press as overnight successes took ten years to get to that point. Ten years. The stories of those businesses always include scary decisions such as selling their homes and living on friends' couches or in the office. You do not have to do that to succeed.

Much of why you are starting this business is for freedom and flexibility, not to go broke or make your life a living hell. Start small, keep the income and insurance for as long as you want to, forever — if that's what you want. There are no rules in tiny businesses, only the path of those before you to help you see what's possible. Your story has not been written yet. You can put whatever you want in it.

Sum It Up:

- Unless you need money, you do not need a business plan to start a business.
- The amount of money you need to launch will depend on what you business is, but stay scrappy! Keep costs as low as possible at the beginning.
- There is no shame in keeping a steady income from a job while you are starting. It can often be an excellent decision mentally, as most businesses take two years to start making enough money for the business and the owner to live off of.

Chapter 11:

Money. You Want to Make It.

To make money, you will have to charge for your goods and services. This means that you will need a way to collect it, a place to store it, and unfortunately if you live in the U.S., you'll give a percentage of it to the U.S. government.[33]

We'll start with collecting it. Once you file your business formation, you can take that stamped document to a bank (look into this, not all banks will open a business account for a DBA, but many do) and open a business checking account. It makes life easier when it comes time to pay taxes to keep your personal and business monies separate and having a business debit/credit card to purchase with. Setting yourself up properly in banking will also be incredibly useful if you reach the point where you want a business loan.

When considering ways to collect money from clients and customers, the important thing to remember is to make it as simple as possible for people to pay you for your goods and

33 https://www.irs.gov/

services. People have a lot going on, if something is annoying or difficult to get, or something becomes complicated, they'll move on. This has been an issue with e-commerce since day one. You need to make sure you are not losing customers and sales because they don't want to deal with your weird payment options or because they cannot pay you with the credit card with the best points or the most open credit. Essentially, you are aiming to remove all points of friction to make the sales process run smoother.

In case it's not obvious, you should not accept only Bitcoin or only cash. I understand that credit card processing takes a fee[34], it's called the cost of doing business. Deal with it and work it into your pricing (and if you're this upset about 3%, wait until we get to income tax!). You will lose customers or not get customers if it's difficult to pay you. Unless you are an exception. Let's not make bets on the chance you are an exception. Aim for low friction.

The great news is that payment gateways are now easier than ever to become approved to use. Hooray! This means that you have options. If you use a bank as your merchant account, such as Chase, you will have to use a gateway that will handle the processing. Usually, authorize.net is the standard. Note that both the merchant account and the gateway account will have

34 Understand and compare credit card processing fees: https://www.fundera.com/blog/credit-card-processing-fees

fees. Or you can use PayPal or Stripe which are all in one and no longer need a gateway. It's up to you what options you offer, but make sure it's something that can grow with you and handle all the ways you provide service to your customers.

To show you what can happen if you are not prepared, we'll return to the Real Simple Guide in 2008. Back in the day, specifically in 2003, when I started my first e-commerce shop, there was no Etsy. Shopping carts had to be coded and they were super simple. You couldn't even process the cards through them. I would receive an email with the full credit card numbers and info. (The thought of how much fraud went down is just wild to think about, and part of why we should all be thankful for the current security measures in place). Anyway, you then had to process the cards in some manner, and for makers, well, banks wouldn't typically talk to you until you had proof of consistent sales and the fees were high, as you know, so was fraud. So many of us were using small processing companies with super low limits.

Fast forward to the fall of 2008. The economy was crashing. That summer my publicist had me do a round of desk sides (I was still in New York where all the magazines were) for the holiday gift guides and had me push a line I had released of these adorable vintage flower cabochons which I turned into earrings. Due to a stroke of luck, $10 gifts were ideal when the economy crashed. Keep in mind that holiday magazines close six months out, so we had no idea when I was told I would be in the Real Simple Holiday Gift Guide that the chaos I had just described was about to happen.

Within a week of the magazine release in the first week of November, I reached the dollar limit on what I could process for credit cards for the month and orders were pouring in. I had no idea how I would even be able to charge the credit cards. And the orders didn't let up, I was getting hundreds a day. I went to my bank, Chase, and explained what was going on. They asked to see proof of orders and I whipped out a printed stack from the last few days that was an entire ream of paper. That proof was all I needed, they approved me for a processing account, with a great rate as I was bringing in such a volume. Luck had struck again, as when that post-holiday volume slowed down, the rate did not! I was able to go home and started manually processing. Which P.S. in those days was such a nightmare, you wouldn't know cards were declined in real-time, so then I would have to email people that their cards were declined and then they would say something like, "impossible!" and we would have to figure out if the numbers were wrong. I am so thankful for the improvements in technology!

The point is that it could have easily shut me down and ruined my business. There are thousands of stories of press hits ruining companies. Don't let yours be one of them and try and prevent something like a website or payment processor ruining your boom.

If you sell a product, make sure you can accept money both online and in person. Even if you don't do shows or go out and sell things if you have a product and someone wants to stop by and pick one up from you, can they? Can you easily accept payment? Venmo and Quick Pay are great options in these cases now and Venmo has begun positioning itself in the business space.

If you sell services, especially if they are over $100, you need to accept credit cards that do not add fees to the client. You are responsible to pay the processing fees, you are the business owner. You should have a way they can easily purchase online and be able to invoice for payments as well. Stripe[35] and Paypal are again great for this. Basically, the more options you have, the more likely you are to make money.

Taxes. You Have to Pay Them.

You will be paying at the very least, federal income tax. I touched on all of this in the chapter, *Am I doing this right?*, but if you are a sole proprietor or DBA, you will file your taxes annually with a 1040 Schedule C.[36] Using something like Turbo Tax will be

35 https://stripe.com/; https://www.paypal.com/; https://venmo.com/

36 See the form and get more info: https://www.irs.gov/forms-pubs/about-sched-

fine to start. The tax identification number you use will be your social security number.

Everyone else will need to file for an EIN, which stands for Employer Identification Number.[37] You will need an EIN if you purchase a going business, are creating a partnership (including if you are changing from a DBA to an LLC) or corporation, or if you hire any employees including household/family members.

If your state requires state income tax, you will need to pay that as well. Included in both federal and state tax, is self-employment tax. As you earn more, you will want to speak with a CPA, or accountant about your business formation to enable you to pay fewer taxes. Before you make decisions on forming a new business entity. Be sure and do your own research to understand what it will mean and what the fees will be. Ask what you will have to pay a tax professional to file and remember that professionals are in business. They may not always have your best interest in mind, it is up to you to have your best interest in and mind. It is also on you to pay for any mistakes made, so you need to know what is going on with your money.

If this is day one and you are not sure you will make any money this year, you're good with a DBA. I say all this not being a financial or tax professional. I am giving you an overview of

---

ule-c-form-1040

37 Apply for an EIN: https://www.irs.gov/businesses/small-businesses-self-employed/apply-for-an-employer-identification-number-ein-online

taxes as a guide. It is on you to research what will work best for you and your business in your state.

When you prepare your taxes, you will have to define your business with a Principle Business Activity Code.[38] These codes classify enterprises and there are many. When you file your taxes with a tax professional or by using tax software, you will be guided through the process of classification.

Tax Deductions aka claims, or "write-offs" are expenses that you can deduct from your taxable income. There is a huge list of deductions possible for small businesses and they change all the time. This is where the experience and knowledge from tax professionals become so valuable as you make and spend more money. As you begin earning more, you will greatly appreciate being advised in these areas. This first year or two, you can use software to lead you through your deductions. To be able to benefit from these, you need to keep all receipts and records of the money that you are spending throughout the year.

Doing a quick Google search will bring up tons of specifics on deductions, but the main categories are:

- Advertising and promotion
- Meals
- Insurance

---

38 The full list of codes is on page 17 and 18: https://www.irs.gov/pub/irs-pdf/i1040sc.pdf

- Bank fees
- Mileage
- Contract labor
- Depreciation (big pieces of equipment or computers are split up over years)
- Education (like this book!)
- Home Office
- Legal and professional fees (like a tax professional)
- Moving expenses
- Rent
- Salaries and benefits
- Taxes and licenses
- Telephone and internet

Depending on your circumstances including your household, you may treat deductions differently than say your best friend does with their business. Year one and two may not be a big deal, but as your income increases or if you need to have proof of income for loans such as buying a car or a home, I strongly suggest you speak with a tax professional in how you file.

Sales tax is a must in most states if you sell a product and likely if you provide services. Sales tax is a *maybe* if you sell something that can be downloaded. In Texas, if you sell a downloadable worksheet, you need to pay sales tax on it. You are also sometimes taxed on services. The laws for sales tax online have been changing as well. It varies from state to state. Please check with your own state laws.

Remember when you opened a business checking account? It may be worth opening at least one savings account to go with that (If you read Profit First, you would know this). You can also use a personal savings account if it's free, but make sure you earmark one solely for your business taxes. Into that account, put all your collected sales tax. That is not your money. Don't make yourself think it is. A wise move is to also take out 25% - 30%[39] off all earned money coming in and put in that tax account as well so when you pay your monthly, quarterly, or annual taxes (depending on how you set it up and your business formation), you have no surprises.

If you move, you need to update all your legal paperwork. If you have a DBA, you must go to the County Clerk in the new county, search your business and register. You must apply for a sales tax permit if you have changed states. You also need to end your sales tax permit in the state you are leaving. Why? If your state and county think you are still doing business, you will accrue fines for not filing and potentially be liable for back taxes. I had this happen to a client, it was not pretty. You do not

39 A good place to begin learning more about small business income tax: https://www.fundera.com/blog/small-business-tax-rate

want to hand your cash flow over to a state you no longer live in for a tax mishap. It could put you out of business. Stay current on your paperwork.

If you change your business name, you also need to update your paperwork with the government. Thanks to Covid, filing has finally caught up to the 21st century, so you can now do most of it online and will take you less than an hour. I recently closed one sales tax account in Texas and opened another all in less than an hour.

Research the laws in your state and county and speak to a tax professional or research for your state and county for any of these specifics. This is the one area where you want to be the most careful and the good news is that it's also the one place where there is a playbook. Do your homework, read before you sign anything, move slowly while filling out the paperwork and you'll do just fine.

Sum It Up:

- You will need a way to accept funds, including from credit cards, from your clients or customers. The easier it is for people to pay you, the better.
- You are responsible for what you pay (and don't pay) for your income taxes. This holds true even if you use a bookkeeper and a CPA. Know your money.

- Sales tax may be required by your state and the different states you sell to. Within states, the rate can change from county to county. Research the rules.

Chapter 12:

More Than a Price Tag

Pricing is one of the conversations that is the most important to have and yet seems to be given the least amount of space. In the beginning, tiny business owners tend to be so focused on getting going that they often vastly underestimate how long it will take for something to gain traction. And they certainly are not thinking about the psychology of pricing or why they should never undersell themselves or price themselves out of their market.

There are a few things we are going to talk about with pricing, including a reality check about if you are making a profit on each product/service. We need to ensure that you can make what you need to make with what you are selling, then we will address the psychology of pricing.

There are many books out there specifically about buyer behavior and the psychology aspect, so we are going to skim on this one. If you want to further explore this topic, my all-time favorite is *Why We Buy* by Paco Underhill. He was the first to research and write about shopping habits and it's fantastic for product-based companies to read. *Selling The Invisible* by Harry Beckwith, although it's nearing "classic" status and parts are outdated, is excellent for service providers. If you are in tech solutions or software, *ReWork* by the Basecamp guys is one of my all-time favorite business books.

Finally, in a chapter on pricing, it would be irresponsible of me not to explain revenue streams and product collections, as they play a big role in keeping the lights on, the cash flowing and a structure for how you can look at your sales cycle.

Where Does What You Charge Come From?

It's ok if when I ask you what you will charge for your widget or service, that you have no idea. We have to start somewhere. Let's, however, put a little thought into this. When, for example, selling handmade items, you could determine your pricing based on materials, time, and overhead. Research the brands that seem like yours and make sure that you're in the right area. Ensure that when you are selling wholesale, you make a profit based on those prices. The additional revenue you make when selling directly to customers is a bonus.

This was how I approached pricing in my jewelry business. About 12 years in, after growing to new levels and transitioning from the indie maker world to the fashion world with a stronger intent, I was introduced to an accessories branding strategist. Why? Because while my jewelry was killing it in the Indie world (does that even exist anymore?) and I had risen to the top of that genre, I was out of my league when I entered the department store retail space (which also barely exists anymore).

Specifically, I was being pitched to one of the big B's in NY by a trend scout and was lucky enough to get my hands on the notes from the buyers after the meeting. The premise was that they liked the designs, but my brand was all over the place. They couldn't tell where I was positioned. I had *no idea* what they were talking about. Although I made it to the pages of all the fashion glossies, I was more loved by the readers of Bust and Venus. I was vastly out of my league in the corporate retail world and yes, my branding was all over the place. I asked the rep for advice and she made a phone call.

Which led me to work with this woman whom I paid a fortune to give me a fast-track education in brand merchandising and retail. In fashion, there are 13 levels of positioning. Where you fit determines your price point, which big stores you would be in and what your branding looks like. I really have to say that in the years since the big stores are all closing, and I hope that this is changing. The indie world was a beautiful place of creativity, community, and few rules. It wasn't until I sat here writing this that I realized that it was when that world basically got bought up by big fashion, that I lost the love for what I did. When art turned to merchandising.

However, if I wanted to keep growing as a jewelry designer, I had to assess the territory and see what the options were. The beauty of tiny is that you often have the freedom to make choices such as where to be, and ultimately, I opted not to pursue any of the big B's: Bergdorf's, Barney's, and Bendel's (which only Bergdorf's is left and that's because it's owned by Neiman Marcus). It was at this time that I also made the decision to remain tiny myself. I did want to have my work manufactured overseas and remove the personal touch. It was against everything I loved about the business I built. But everyone I turned to for advice said I would not "be successful" if I did not grow to this level.

The experiences during these years are why I do what I do now. **I will repeat it again, you can have an incredible business with 5 or fewer employees. And it's up to you to decide what success means to you and your business.**

The real point here, however depressing it is, is that no matter what your industry, there are different levels of price, or positioning that decide how you will be perceived in your industry based on where you are positioned. If you set yourself out to be the most competitive on price, i.e., the cheapest, you will lose. Try to avoid that from day one. Besides the lowest level of price, there is always a variety of levels of pricing within each industry, you do have options.

How do you choose? As much as you want to avoid the lowest price level, you should probably for now, not be the highest unless you have the experience to justify it. If you are a product and want to start luxe, make sure your materials are luxe and go for it. Make sure you are meticulous with your branding. Entering the market in the middle pricing is never a bad way to start.

How will you know what the market is? You will need to research who you believe your competitors are and what they charge. This is not a 10-minute exercise. You should spend a good amount of time on this before you get out there. I would spend a few hours, spread out over a couple of weeks on this. Have at least 10 if not 20 businesses in your space who you discover in your research. They should include a range of experienced and new businesses in the market and one or two should be from the top, the big names people think of in your market. They can be in your town, in different locations, and with different and similar niches. You should know inside and out who they are, what they offer, what they charge and how they position themselves.

Every time you want to release a new revenue stream, you will repeat this exercise and review these companies and what they do. Redesigning your webpage? Repeat this exercise. Knowing what you do not want to be is as important as knowing what you do want to be.

While researching it is imperative to remember that those who have been in business for 15+ years are not where you will be at the beginning. Remind yourself of this daily. You may strive to be where they are, but not for today. Do not compare your step A to their Z.

Why do you have to know all of this? Because competition makes us stronger. It pushes us to be better and serve our customers and clients well, but also because you want a differentiator. There are over 14,000 licensed Realtors in the Austin, TX area.[40] Sure, many of them probably don't have much success, but 2,800 are in the top 20% and considered successful. Guess what, all 2,800 are in the top 20% and doing great! There is plenty out there for everyone. Don't think you have to reinvent the wheel, but you should know what makes your wheel unique and why people would want to have your wheel instead of all the other wheels.

This is called a USP: Unique Selling Proposition and it's wildly important in marketing. Understanding your USP from the beginning will be immensely helpful, even if you change all your branding and positioning later. Think of all the skills

---

40 https://www.abor.com/

you bring to the table. Those skills are stacked up, and are what make *you* unique.

There is no shame in change. If you start out and realize that you are going in the wrong direction, no big deal. You are a tiny business owner; you can move fast and adapt. It's part of your superpower skill set!

When you begin, start with your step A. You want to begin by focusing on one service, one offer, or one collection. You are not launching with all that Amazon carries. Jeff Bezos only had one thing at the beginning, he sold books. It was years before he had the everything store.

Select the thing you want to start with, do your research on your market, decide on a price and go tell people about it. Get someone to pay you for it. At this point, you don't need a website, your prices printed anywhere, or anything fancy. Some business cards would be a good idea if you will see people in person. Canva is an incredibly easy way to design great cards and offers printing services. If you sell products, start with an Etsy shop if you're a maker or Amazon if you're not. Start small so you can adapt and grow!

Branding

When you first get started, your branding is not as important as you think it is. Why? Because you will most likely be evolving over the first year or two as you figure out more of what you offer, who you are targeting and your price points. Getting a logo made is often the first thing people do when they start their business. And often they spend hundreds of dollars in doing so. This is necessary for some businesses, such as a brick n mortar, but if you are creating products to sell online, or offering services, it's not the priority. Often, you will save money and stress if you wait a bit to understand who is paying for your products and services and what you want to offer before you hire a graphic designer.

For the first few months, as you figure things out, you can use Canva to design something of your own or hire on Fiver or Etsy to design a logo for under $100. Remember, you can change this as you grow, it does not need to be perfect. You do not have to have expensive branding from day one. You do not need a $2000 logo the minute you open an Etsy shop. If someone tells you that you must, look into if they are selling branding services and realize that they too are a business trying to sell their services. In fact, chances are you will change your branding and logo at some point if you are in business for over 5 years.

In the 16 years I had a jewelry brand, I changed my logo 3 times. I created the first logo myself, but as I was growing and evolving, I hired branding experts to help me pivot to the next levels. The first thing they would say is, you need a new logo and branding. Everything changed at those times, but in between, I would update the look of my website every year and have new images created quarterly for the collections with both product and lifestyle shots. Those images were just as important as my logo. Those images represent your products (and your brand) and will determine if people will buy from you more than a logo would. And those will evolve too!

Do a quick search on logos through the years and you'll realize that many of your favorite brands have changed their logos a handful of times. They have also changed their taglines, fonts, and colors. It's ok to evolve, start simple, small, and inexpensive and expand as you make more money.

When you are ready to get your branding together, what do you need to start?

- The name!
- Your domain name and setting up an email with yourname@yourdomain.com (you can set up the email through Gmail or Outlook).
- Your social media handles which all match.
- A logo. You do not need to spend thousands on your logo at the beginning. You can use logo designers on Etsy. Fiverr works too, but they are rarely in the U.S.

so communication hours and getting your point across clearly can be difficult. You can barter with a graphic designer friend. Ask in your network. Make sure you look at their work and like their style. They are designers, you want to like their designs. You want to make sure they work with tiny businesses, so you are not paying them crazy amounts of money.

- Business cards. Yes, many people still ask for them.
- Two colors. Research brand colors to see the psychology of color in branding.
- Your preferred text color (a deep, dark almost black but not black).
- A serif and sans serif font to use on your website and anything printed or typed. You can search font sets and see which ones typically work together.
- A headshot.
- Images of your products if you offer them.
- Lifestyle shots for your website. You can use stock images from Canva, Unsplash, Pixaby, or Pexels.[41]

Learn how to take product shots yourself. Research what you need and how to do it. To start you can use natural light

41 https://www.canva.com/, https://unsplash.com/, https://pixabay.com/, https://www.pexels.com/

outside at the "magic hours" of dusk and dawn and a neutral or background. You can build a lightbox from foam core or order a collapsible one. You can order faux marble backdrops. I was at a shoot at Time Out New York years ago and they told me to buy a white sheet of plexiglass or acrylic. I bought a 12" x 12" one for under $30 and used it for a decade to shoot my jewelry on. It costs a fortune to have product shots taken. In 16 years, I never hired out my product shots (ok, I tried once and I confirmed never to do that again). I took my own every season. I did hire out photoshoots with models, but product shots, I did all on my own. You can too with practice, especially year one. At the very least, try to do it. That's it for branding materials at the beginning.

The biggest branding expense will be your website. I highly recommend that at the early stage, you try and design your own website. It's easy to spend $5000+ on a beautiful website and it will look great! But most tiny businesses change so much in the first year that you will need to be updating constantly and that first version may only be used for a few months if you shift your branding or what you offer. You will also have to pay someone to do all minor updates and that can get crazy expensive fast. Shopify, Squarespace, and Wix[42] are all great options with SEO benefits that you can use to create your own website.

---

42 https://www.shopify.com/, https://www.squarespace.com/, https://www.wix.com/

Once you have a firm grasp of what you are selling and who you are selling to, then you can bring in the hired website designers. If you have been doing it yourself to this point, it will help them understand what your needs are. Again, note that when looking for website designers, those who work with "small businesses" typically mean much larger than a tiny business. A full-service design can easily run $25k. Look for designers who work with tiny business owners, ask for referrals. Many designers have niches, look for the ones who specialize in yours.

It's good to be aware that the business model of website designers usually includes the maintenance fee on a monthly level. For those of you who are starting a web design company, this is a great idea. For those of you hiring to have someone design your website, this can add up quickly so be aware of these costs before you jump into a contract.

Speaking of that, a small side note is that if you are using Gmail or Outlook for your business, this is where you do need to pay for the monthly fee from day one. The policies on these accounts are that if there is a problem, they provide zero help on free accounts. This means that if you lose your email, you may lose everything attached to it, like social media accounts and stores. This can be a nightmare, even if it's for a few days. The $8-$10 a month paying for these platforms is beyond worth it in protection. (This is a tip from my friend, Richard Avery, a cybersecurity expert and owner of Titanium Computing[43])

To understand how to brand yourself according to your position in the market, this is where your research on your competitors comes into play. It's also why it's so important to know your person. You are going to look at the brands you are competing against and that your person uses, and you are going to make sure that you are in alignment with their pricing and branding. Think about when you are advertised to on Facebook. You see something and you're like, "Oh, that's totally my style, I'll check that out." It's because your previous shopping and viewing patterns have triggered the algorithm to show you new brands that match the positioning of what you like. You want people to have the same reaction to your branding when they see it.

Your colors, fonts, and images will all help you in targeting your person and make them think, "I like that, and it's perfect for *me*!" and then click BUY.

Understanding Overhead

A big thing you need to keep in mind when setting your pricing is that what you charge for your product or service is responsible for paying for more than your time. It's paying for the materials, the time to make it or buy it, all of the business expenses, taxes, and to pay anyone who works for you. That's a lot to come of

43 Richard is a wealth of knowledge: https://www.titaniumcomputing.com/

the price of one widget or hour of service.

When you get paid in a job, you only are removing the taxes and perhaps paying yourself first through retirement and savings. The rest is yours to keep. When you own a business, there is a much smaller percentage of each dollar earned that goes into your pocket. And then there is the time issue. Most people who do hourly consulting or coaching can fit about 20 hours per week into their schedule of client work. You typically have an hour of work in addition to each hour you are charging for. That work includes invoicing, sales, notes, marketing, etc. When setting your prices, you need to keep things like this in mind or you will quickly be out of cash and out of business.

There are many ways to determine pricing and many opinions on how it should be done. This proves that there is once again no one, exact, perfect way to do something. You want to find a way that works well for you, but keep in mind that with any price, you are aiming for a high-profit margin.

There are, of course, many ways to calculate margins. You want to look at gross margins and net margins and there are different reasons to look at both. Basically, Gross margins are the money you make with the cost of goods removed. This number is helpful to determine if your products are worth selling. Net margins are the money you have left after everything comes out or, your earnings once the expenses are deducted. Net Margin is the measure of the profitability of your business and its financial health.

You want to have money left over after you remove all expenses and business costs. The best way to ensure this is to make sure that you are making a strong profit when you sell your goods and services. You don't want to have super low margins on a product, or you'll have to sell crazy high numbers to make a profit, and that is incredibly difficult as a tiny business. You can always try and improve margins on products by purchasing a higher quantity of supplies to get a lower price. Sometimes teaming up with a fellow maker can get you there if you order raw materials together, but you still have to sell more to buy more, so beware of that game too early.

The same goes for service-based businesses. If you charge $25/hour and can bill 20 hours a week, that means that the gross income is $500. Subtract taxes and you're down to $400 or $375. Remove overhead and you may not have made any money. See why this is important to pay attention to?

Besides your market research, understanding your competitors and what the market will bear, it's important to have an idea of how much money you need to earn in your first year of FULL business and what you need now. Remember that you probably won't get to your ideal earning number for two years. If you can live on nothing now and have money to put into the business, that's great, but if you need to have cash coming in, then you need to be realistic. Maybe you realize that you need to keep a full-time job or get a side job for a few years. There is no shame in this! It is much better to be prepared for reality than to be delusional and unable to eat and pay rent.

Each year, you should increase your prices. If you do it annually, there will be no scary jump. Increase in small increments. An annual increase of 5-10% will cover the rate of inflation and not freak out your clients and customers.

A note on how to know if you are charging too high or too low. Pitch to 5 solid leads. If 5 say yes, your prices are too low. If 5 say no, they're too high (or you're not explaining the value well enough or your positioning is off for your pricing). If 2 or 3 say yes, you're just right.

Profit

In the past few years, with the rise of tech startups and the tech enterprises buying up startups, there seems to be a weird philosophy forming that profit doesn't matter. Let's talk about that for a minute. Yes, there are instances where profit doesn't matter. Those instances are when they are a company that is focused on scaling at a rapid rate and proving that the potential users are out there. They have structured the business on getting as many people signed up for a free product as possible with the hopes to sell or go public in the near future.

Some of these models are created as Freemiums, which basically means that there is tiered subscription pricing, and the paid versions have more options which they will push on you to upgrade. Most apps and software use this model. Some want to be a subscription-based model with no annual option, they simply want you to pay monthly forever (hello, Netflix), some are a mix and want to have a huge number of users so they can charge for ads to cover the costs. Many of the big podcasts fall under this. And then there are the hybrids where they have ads and then a subscription version that is ad-free. The language app Duolingo[44] has this model and a scant 1.75% of the users pay for the ad-free subscription which in early 2020 was over 1 million users. They have such massive numbers that this model is possible and in addition to the subscribers, the free version has ads, creating additional revenue.

That is an exciting example, but incredibly rare. Unless you are one of these types of tech startups, you will need to make a profit and have cash flow, or you will be one of the large percentages of businesses that do not make it. As we discussed earlier, the number one reason businesses fail is due to lack of cash flow.

You want to make sure that you are charging a fair price that

---

44 Learn a language in 15 minutes a day: https://www.duolingo.com/

allows you to profit. Maybe not enough in the first two years to live off at the amount you used to earn at a job, but enough to start to grow the business and pay yourself at all. Besides pricing, the best way to achieve this is to stay scrappy. Start with the free (the freemium version!) version with everything you use when possible and pay only when it impedes your progress. This applies to apps, workspaces, technology, and really to everything. Use what you've got until it's painful not to pay for something. Don't buy things before you need them, especially technology.

For the first two years, you want to keep your overhead as low as possible, so that whatever is coming in, is not immediately gobbled up by overhead costs. Stay scrappy and focus on selling.

Once you do start to bring in more revenue, make sure you are padding the future before you start to spend. First, upgrade the necessary tech and then try and put aside a few months of business savings. Then if you still have more money than you know what to do with, look at where you can put money to help you grow. I have made some of the stupidest business decisions in these situations. Paying for "services" that I did not research well enough because I had extra money and thought, why not try it? Thousands of dollars given to pray and spray Robo services. I would get all excited when I would seek out help and something would work, that I would let my guard down and sign up for the next three things that came my way, hoping to replicate how awesome that first thing was. This was a horrible strategy.

A word on SEO as this is one of the first services that comes up when business owners start making some money and are looking for business solutions. I asked experts in the SEO space. I was told more than once that if a company proposes they can make a difference in your business if you subscribe to their monthly service and it is less than $5,000 a month for at least 6 months and is not specialized for your business, it will do nothing. That's a great problem to solve, by the way, if someone can figure out how to help tiny businesses without just scamming them.

A great rule of thumb? If it sounds too good to be true? If the person has reached out to you to tell you about how much their service can help you? If you are really receiving a stealth email with an unsubscribe at the bottom? Ignore it. If you are looking for great services, for people who can use their skills to help your business? Ask your network. Ask for referrals from people you trust. This is one of the reasons why networking is not an icky thing and it's essential to your success!

Paying Yourself First

Income tax, sales tax, and property taxes. You must pay them. In some states, a bit less in certain areas, more in others, but as there is federal income tax in the U.S., you are paying taxes no matter what. Plan for it. Open a savings account and every time money comes in, put 30% in that account. 40% if you are in a higher tax bracket. If you don't need it all when it's time to pay taxes, excellent, but better to have extra, than not enough. Although if you don't have the money on hand, do not ignore the IRS! Call them and set up a payment plan.

Another great philosophy with business income is to pay yourself first. After taxes, have money automatically put aside each week/month/quarter depending on how reliable your income is, into savings accounts or directly into the specific accounts for your retirement (Roth or SEP IRAs) and any insurance you need. Next would be a savings account for you personally and then your business for emergencies. Your personal emergency fund should have 3-6 months' income. Business ideally 3 - 6 months of business operating costs. Then hack away at any debt.

Sum It Up:

- Pricing is part of branding and will be determined by your market and your position in the market. Where and how you put yourself will influence how high you can price.
- When selecting the elements for your branding, stay scrappy! DIY as much as you can for the first few months and upgrade as your profits increase.

- Keep your overhead low and maximize your profits as you grow, cash flow is essential to survival, as is paying yourself.

Chapter 13:

Beginning at Zero

Analytics and data tracking are wonderful tools to help you understand your business. When you first open your doors, there is not much to collect, which means you may not think to start tracking. Once you start to collect and track, it typically will take two years of data and numbers to start to really see patterns and be able to use the data well. But the earlier you start to set up systems for collecting, the sooner you can make use of these patterns. The longer you wait to start collecting data, the longer you'll have to wait to start analyzing and some of the data you'll want to collect can be useful after a month.

Let's begin with what will make your life easier and your business stronger. The very first thing you can do if you have even a simple landing page on your URL is to set up Google Analytics.[45] Before you get busy is a great time to set it up as you may not have a ton of clients or sales yet, so you'll have time to learn how it will work for you. You can use your Google

45 https://analytics.google.com/analytics/web/

Analytics (it's free) account to track everything from traffic to conversions to demographics. It's the most important data you will collect online. They have their own little virtual Academy[46] and plenty of resources to help you out. You can simply Google what you use to host your website "and Google Analytics", and the instructions will pop up. For example type "Wix and Google Analytics" and instructions will be the first thing to pop up.

If you are using social media for your marketing, switch all your accounts over to business accounts. These are also free and will enable you to access stats in your accounts and will be invaluable as you grow. It will also be a fantastic resource to make sure you are really reaching the people you want and to make sure you understand who your customers are. Many times, we declare who our "person" is only to later realize that we were off on their age by about 20 years because we guessed. Guessing will only get you so far in marketing.

Let's now talk about something that seems so simple (and maybe the words boring, or unnecessary come up) but incredibly useful and can be free to use: Spreadsheets. All you really need to track data is a simple spreadsheet. I enjoy Excel, you may prefer Google or something from Apple, but no matter what application you use, a simple spreadsheet is the ideal alternative to a host of fancy and expensive apps to track data. As always,

---

46 https://analytics.google.com/analytics/academy/

start scrappy and free and use what you are already paying for.

If you are struggling to set up something useful, Etsy is a fantastic place to buy reasonably priced templates already set up for a variety of your needs. You can also Google them, but Etsy seems to have just enough options that it's not overwhelming when you search. You also can use the Microsoft templates in Excel if you subscribe to Microsoft Office.

Tracking Money

Let's get deeper into tracking your sales and expenses. What numbers are we looking to collect and why? Besides the obvious things such as tracking income to pay the correct amount of taxes, we want to also start keeping an eye on a few things.

First, we want to look at what sells well. If you have a few different products, services, or revenue streams, it's great to see what does well so we know what to do more of and what to do less of. Know that the Pareto principle of 80/20 is typically true with sales, you will make 80% of your sales from 20% of your offerings, so don't immediately get discouraged by things not selling as well as others. You may have higher-end products that never sell but attract press and web traffic, so they are worth keeping for other reasons. You also want to have a range of prices in your offerings to push sales towards your mid-range pricing. So you don't want to remove things simply due to not selling well, but it is important to know what does sell well.

The second is customer/client behavior. How much do your customers tend to spend on their first purchase? Do they return and if so, after how long and how much are they spending? What is their average purchase amount? What is their lifetime value? What products and services are they buying and in what order? This is all incredibly important, so in the future, you'll know what to spend on acquisition. Again, these numbers will be the most useful after two years of data, but great to start collecting from the beginning.

Third, we want to make sure it's possible to make the amount of money we will need to run the business and pay ourselves what we want to be making. Many people set out to make what they made from their day job and need to reach a specific number to leave that job. Having a crystal-clear understanding of this will make sure you are not leaving your job too soon.

If you are quickly filling up your hours with consulting and are realizing that at the rate you are charging, it will be impossible to work the number of hours you need to hit that magic number, then you need to adjust your pricing or add in revenue streams. As you are calculating what you will need to charge, understand that typically for an hour of consulting, you will do an additional hour of work. Meaning that if you want to work 40 hours and have 20 one-hour client sessions, all you will have time for is to meet with those 20 clients each week and the prep/follow-up work. There will be no time for networking, no time for researching, no time for anything except clients.

Last is the expenses piece. This is where you'll be glad that you're scrappy as it adds up fast! Don't be scrappy at your own detriment but be realistic about how much needs to come in to cover what needs to go out. Office supplies are cheaper if you buy them in bulk, but if it takes you years to use the 1,000 pens you purchased and by the time you use them, they have dried out, it's not worth the cost. You will use these numbers for your taxes as well, so it's easiest to keep up with receipts as you go instead of all at once at the end of the year. Your expenses determine as much of your cash flow as your income does, so it's crucial to understand what goes out as much as what is coming in.

Tracking Clients and Customers

Now for the people tracking part using a spreadsheet or a CRM solution. CRM stands for Client Relationship Management. You can be as simple or as complicated as you want here. Most CRM software solutions are designed for teams and you are paying for the ability to use them for a team. If you decide to use this software and not a spreadsheet, be sure to research options for small businesses. There are also many solutions that have been created specifically for different industries, be it photographers or realtors. For now, a simple spreadsheet can work beautifully.

When we talk about what gets input on that CRM, we are talking about tracking your actual relationships and transactions. Not correspondence through a newsletter. If you have an email list, this is something different and I urge that you right away begin using an email solution to manage those. It's just easier to track unsubscribes and to avoid spamming people. There are many services, such as Mailchimp[47], that have great free versions for up to 2000 contacts. Allow something like Mailchimp to be in charge of your list so you don't have to deal with the risk of having your email blacklisted for spam.[48]

CRM's are for your networking contacts, your sales leads, and prospecting contacts. These are different contacts than those who will be on your mailing list. This is important to understand. You are not allowed to add people you meet networking to your email list without explicit permission. That is SPAM and you can have your email address blacklisted for it, there are laws around this now. If you are sending a broad email out to people without their permission, you also must give them a way to opt-out and unsubscribe.

As for your contacts and leads, a nice spreadsheet is sufficient. You want to include their contact info, where you met them and ideally, a pattern of contact for staying in touch with those with

---

47 https://mailchimp.com/

48 Everything you have ever wondered about Spam (not the canned ham): https://www.consumer.ftc.gov/topics/online-security

who you want to have relationships (I enjoy quarterly).

Ideally, you would create a second spreadsheet for clients so you can further track their purchasing patterns and make sure you are staying in touch with them as well. Include where you met them (so you know the best lead sources), when what and how much they purchase and any details. Details such as birthdays or their kids' names, really, anything that you want to stay on top of. Always include as much contact info possible as well.

Tracking leads is the best way to know which efforts in getting them are working, which efforts are not and what needs to be followed up on.

Tracking Your Marketing

As far as marketing goes, you want to collect data on the basic stats, but not drive yourself crazy with too many details. Again, a simple spreadsheet to track your followers and engagement with each social media outlet, your blog, and content channels such as medium or YouTube. This will help to measure metrics in a nice overview without becoming obsessive or time-consuming to manage.

When considering what and how often to track, you can get as in-depth or as broad as you feel helps you to know what to focus on and where to spend your time. If you are advertising or spending money on your marketing, then having a way to track that as well will help you have a better understanding of what works and what does not.

In the 1930's, a concept was created called the Rule of 7. It dictated that people had to be touched by your marketing message seven times before they made a purchase. Now with the fast-paced and saturated world we live in, it's increased to anywhere from 11 to 20+ times, depending on who you ask. You may have no way of knowing where they found you and they may not know either. That's the tricky part of advertising, you really don't know what works unless it's a huge and obvious bump in traffic and sales.

Most of the tracking you are doing with your marketing will be through Google Analytics and your social profile stats. With Google Analytics, watch for sources of traffic, bounce rates, conversions, time spent on site, and demographics. You also can track landing pages, most viewed pages, and other behaviors as well. Again. I recommend spending some time on learning and understanding Google Analytics as it will serve you well!

In your social media accounts, pay attention to what content gets the highest engagement (clicks, likes, and comments), the best times that your audience engages the most and, of course, demographics. If you are finding that one of your three social media channels where you are focusing is just not getting traction, not having any ROI, or not attracting the right audience after six months, stop focusing on it and move on to something else. You will leave that account there, just simply stop putting so much time into it. You can try posting once or twice a month if you want to, but if you remove the link from your website, no one will go to it thinking it should be busy.

Spreadsheets

Now it's time to set up your spreadsheets!

- If opening a blank spreadsheet terrifies you about what to do with it, get yourself templates. Start by opening your search engine (or Etsy) and typing "business spreadsheet templates excel" replacing of course excel with an alternative if need be. You'll see tons of things come up from project management to income.
- To get started, select templates for your Income, Expenses, CRM, or Clients and Social Media.
- Modify them to suit your needs.
- Schedule a time each month or week to fill in.
- Enjoy the data and having your systems already in place!

Sum It Up:

- Setting up data collection and analytics in the beginning can greatly help you do more of what works and less of what does not.
- Simple spreadsheets are all you need to get going in the beginning.
- Focus on your marketing, clients/leads, and finances to start.

PART III:

Living in Your Business

Chapter 14:

Show Up. Follow Through. Do The Work.

What does it mean to show up, follow-through, and do the work? *It* won't work if *you* don't work. These three things are the backbone to survival and success as a tiny business owner. It sounds easy enough, and in theory, it is, but if you stop doing these simple things, you will struggle to get traction. Let's break them down and then look at how they work together.

What is showing up? Showing up is going to, doing, getting involved, taking the risk, overcoming the fear, and trying new things. Now, I will admit that I, just as much as anybody else, really enjoy the times that I say no, that I don't go, that I decided that I'd rather sit at home than do the thing. But the big question is: do I really enjoy not doing the thing or am I just either fearing a new experience (and by when I say I, I mean many all of us) or am I glad to not have to put real clothes and makeup on and leave the house? But what am I doing by not showing up? Or if I did show up more, what would happen? Do the negatives of not showing up outweigh the thrill of not going?

A great example of showing up is if you have announced a date for launching a new product and you don't make the deadline. How do you feel about that? Setting a deadline and launching when you say you're going to is a huge, huge factor in success. You are setting an example to people about how you are true to your word. You are showing them that they can trust you.

As you're beginning to understand, there are a lot of different ways that you can show up beyond physically being in a place. Let's go deeper with that networking event example. As we all know, networking events can be lame. When you're trying to find a networking group that you want to be a part of, you should take the time to date the group before you join. Attend a few groups and a variety of their events and figure out which one makes you feel comfortable, where you want to spend your time, where the people are who you want to get to know better. The goal is to find a group whose events you do not dread attending and that you look forward to going to.

Taking the time to find a group you like will go a long way in not feeling lame. Networking groups vary in their purpose, style, meeting types, and times. What I've learned for myself is that the evening networking events are not my happy place. I really enjoy my evening ritual of working on a jigsaw puzzle while listening to podcasts to wind down. If I am instead, at a networking event, I'm sad the whole time about not puzzling.

I'll admit that even if it's a morning event, when it comes time to leave my house, I never want to go. A hack I use to get myself to show up to these things is to take that step to sign up and put it on my schedule. If I sign up, I will go. That's what it means to show up. That if you say you're going to go, go.

For me, a large part of showing up often is to go to a networking event early in the morning. At least there will be coffee and I'll have that to help me extrovert (yes, it's now a verb). Sometimes it's as simple as tweaking the time of day that you say you're going to go to things. If you know you're not going to want to leave your house once you get home from work, don't say yes to evening events, and stick to ones that meet earlier in the day. Set yourself up for success, not failure.

If you are asked to attend by a friend or someone in the group, you simply tell them, "I'm unable to go, that time does not work for me." You don't have to give a reason. You're most likely saying yes to avoid an uncomfortable 30-second conversation and then you figure you just won't show up. Not showing up when you have said you would, can harm your reputation. Explaining that you have a time conflict will do nothing to make people not trust your word. Have a 30-second uncomfortable conversation instead of not showing up. When you say you're going to go, you go. If you say you will not be going, there's no problem whatsoever. Only RSVP yes to the things you plan on attending.

What is follow-through? Doing what you tell people you'll do. Sending the reply or being reliable. Some examples of that would be if you say to somebody, "Oh, I'll send you that report." Then you send the report within 24 hours. Or if you tell someone, "I'll send you an email later today and we'll connect and make a coffee appointment." You need to send that email. It seems so obvious when you write it out. Not a hard thing to wrap your head around, but you need to do it. Surprisingly, a lot of people do not.

If you say you're going to do a task, do the task. If you have started a project, finish the project, unless you know for some reason it is better that you don't finish the project and you know that it is something you should stop working on (this is a different conversation for another time). If you start something, finish it. If you say you're going to do the thing then do the thing. That is follow-through. It is shocking how many people do not follow through, you don't want to be one of those people.

The last is to do the work. What is doing the work? It's sitting down and doing the actual work, not talking about the work, not daydreaming about the work, not procrastinating, not reading about doing the work, not planning around doing the work, but doing the work. Examples of this are to actually write the book, start the podcast, launch the product, kick the bad habit, go to the gym. These things are doing the work. You must do the actual work or there is no thing. There is only an idea.

Why are these three things so important? Well, although not a great person, Woody Allen said a very great thing about this, which is that "80% of success is showing up". If you don't show up, you may not catch the opportunities that could come to you. That's a big deal. I was thinking the other day, I have a bunch of speaking engagements coming up. I have a mastermind that I'm co-hosting with a therapist. I'm going to be leading something at a summit. I was thinking about how these things all came to be. I realized all of them in some way we're impacted by the number of people that I've met through networking. I have all these cool opportunities to grow my business because I am out there and I'm meeting people.

Is it luck or hard work that gets you things? I'll believe a lot of it is luck and a lot of people attribute success to luck, but if you're not there when luck and opportunity come to you, then where does that get you? You need to be top of mind when the person with the opportunity looks for someone to do the thing. You need to be in the right place at the right time to connect with the right people.

Years ago, when I was still a jewelry designer and maker,

a friend called one day and said she passed my name on to one of the shopping channels. They had reached out to her, a DIY expert, host and former jewelry designer, to create a DIY Jewelry show with them. It involved designing jewelry making kits, creating instructional videos and then being on air live for a 2-hour show each week to demonstrate while a shopping channel host sold the materials being used. Based 100% on her reputation and referral, I was asked to interview.

The programs guy at the channel loved me and declared that I was a natural for live TV. The interview was about 15 minutes, and then I had my own TV show. All because I was top of mind and was known for showing up, following through and doing the work. After a year, I opted to not continue as it took a crazy amount of time and was not the path I wanted to pursue, but I learned so much and loved the experience. I'm so happy I was considered for it!

You know the age-old adage, it's who you know, not what you know? Well, you need to go out and meet these people and form relationships, so they know you, trust you, and like you. With success, relationships are everything. If you're building a business, relationships are gold and if you're showing up repeatedly for them, you are building relationships. If you tell them you're going to go there and you're there, you're building trust. You're showing that you respect them.

Here's an example of how you are innocently not showing up. At this time everybody creates Facebook events and then invites all their friends. You select going, and maybe you do this with no intention of going, but to help raise awareness for the event. I'll let you in on a little secret. If you mark it as interested instead, it will do just as much and you're not sending an empty promise. You are helping your friend, but you are not promising to be there and then not showing up. Even if you're just marking it as going to be supportive, but you live in another state and you're thinking, of course, they know you're not coming. They'll wonder if there is a chance and when you don't, they're disappointed in you.

Let's continue with the follow-through. It's different from following up. That's what you should be doing after sales calls or if you're trying to get in touch with somebody or something like that. But I'm talking about the really basic concept of follow-through. If you say you're going to do something, you do it. The bottom line is that by following through, you're showing them that you respect them, and it builds trust.

For years, I was incredibly involved in the National MS Society and I chaired a committee for a big event that we have here in Texas. When I would gather my new committee at the start of our year my favorite thing to do is to go around the room of 25 to 30 of us and ask everyone their biggest pet peeve about working in groups was. Sometimes it would take a couple of people for it to be said, but as soon as somebody did say this, every single person in that room would say they changed their answer. It's when somebody doesn't follow through with what they said they would do. That would always end up being the biggest pet peeve of every single person in that room.

And because this was a volunteer committee for a great cause, you can imagine that it attracted the brightest and the best of people out there. People who are great at what they do and are very committed to their work. People who regularly show up, follow through and do the work. I feel like that says a lot. I would just like to put that out there as a great example that when you have 30 people that say, my biggest pet peeve is when people don't follow through. A lot of people aren't following through and it's really affecting the success they have in life.

The third one is doing the work. There is a fabulous book called *Do The Work* by Steven Pressfield. It's a quick read, and a great little book to have and to browse through when you're not feeling very motivated. In it, he talks about resistance, that you need to fight through your resistance and do the work. That the resistance is fear and that the fear never goes away. You have to do the work and when you're done doing the work, do more work.

Much of what Pressfield is talking about is geared towards writers and he points out that ideas are worthless if you're not writing the book that you're talking about writing. If you're not writing it, there is no book. You're not an author until there is a book. You have to do the work; you have to write the book. There is currently a weird social media driven perspective of work. It's easy to look at people and get the wrong idea of what their life is like. I guarantee you that people on social media who are successful at their work are not actually lounging by the pool all day. That is not reality. The reality is that it takes a lot of hard work and it takes doing the work to be successful. Once you have done the work, then you get pool time, but pool time alone will not make you successful.

Maybe you've heard of the 10,000-hour rule that Malcolm Gladwell talked about in *Outliers*? Many people loudly don't agree with it. And some people really believe in it. I will say that the people that don't agree with it are basically saying that you can master something faster than in 10,000 hours. That's all they're saying. As Gladwell does point out, you can also put 10,000 hours in and not master something. You will not become world-class at something if you're not constantly improving and working at improving. If you're just mindlessly plugging in the hours and not really giving it your all, then you're not going to achieve that level of world-class.

The premise of the 10,000-hour rule is that if you put in deliberate practice, which breaks down to about three hours a day, you can accomplish mastery in about 9 years. His point is made around music and instruments. You can easily imagine that a world-class cellist probably has been playing since they were four or five years old. That would mean that by the time that they're a teenager, they have practiced for three hours a day and put in that 10,000 hours and they have become world-class at it.

As adults, we want faster success. It's never quick enough for any of us. We all want instant gratification. But you start to see why there is some importance in that 10,000 hours of deliberate practice. In my former career in jewelry design, I was a jewelry designer professionally for almost 16 years. But I started designing and making jewelry when I was probably 15 and started the business at 25. I had almost put in my 10,000 hours before I got to the point where I had cohesive enough designs to make a line and start selling collections. First, I had to put the time in and make something that people wanted to support and put their own hard-earned money into because nobody wants the stuff that you're first learning on. They want your world-class products.

As you start on the journey to creating your business, it is so important to do three simple things. Show up, follow through and do the work. You don't need money to do any of these things. You do need time to do the work, but I guarantee you,

you can find the time. Maybe you can watch one less episode of that Netflix show or get up an hour earlier? But showing up, what does that require?

There are so many instances that I know we've all been through where you drag yourself to the thing that you know you said you were going to go to. You force yourself to do it and you get there. And I bet it's a low percentage that when you get there and after you do the thing, you regret going. Yes, that happens. Of course, it happens, but it's rare to go to the thing and then regret going. Typically, you're happy that you dragged yourself out of the house.

The biggest thing you can do for your success really in anything is to be consistent. When you're there, how often you're there and when you tell somebody you're going to be there, to be there. If you start a blog, you don't have to blog every day, you don't even have to blog every week. But if you say that you're going to blog the third Tuesday of the month, every single third Tuesday of the month, you better have a blog post out and not one of the "Oh, I missed three months, I'm so sorry" posts. If you don't, people will stop coming back to read you because they won't trust you. They'll know that they can't rely on you showing up. You don't have follow-through, and you didn't do the work. It's such a beautiful example. It's like a little ribbon put on the package of why it's important to do those three things.

If every single week you show up, write the blog post, have it up when you say it's going to be up there and do the work to do the blog posts, guess what? You're going to have way more success than if you did not do all those three things together. Start to think about how you can show up, follow through and do the work in your business.

Sum It Up:

- You will be bombarded with opportunities to attend events and be involved as a business owner. Remember that people pay just as much attention to those who say they will come, yet never attend to those who say no. Both people stop being invited. Sign up to go, and actually show up. It's an indication of your integrity.
- If you say you will do something, like making a connection, sending an email, or doing something — do it. Follow through is incredibly important in building relationships.
- You will have to do the work. You can plan all you want, but if you don't actually do the work, you have nothing.

Chapter 15:

Embracing the Slow

I still to this day have a hard time with slow seasons and I have been self-employed for 20 years. They still somehow sneak up and surprise me and give me a lot of anxiety. I know, I know, I'm going to talk about how you're supposed to know these things and be okay, but it's still hard. Understand that I struggle with this too. I'm not saying that you shouldn't struggle with it, but I am going to give you some tips for how, perhaps, you can maybe not feel so freaked out. First, let's talk about how you can figure out when your slow season is. Then we'll cover some things that you can do to make slow times useful.

The easiest way to see when your slow season is is to look at multiple past years and compare what has happened in the past to where you are now. If you are new to business, that is impossible because you have nothing to compare it to. Then what are you supposed to do? Well, you do not live in a bubble. There are other businesses out there just like yours. Do some research. Talk to people who are in the same business or field. Find out what other people are going through. I promise you that you're not alone. That's the beauty of this big world that we live in. There are people that are going through things, just like you. Reach out to your network, join some Facebook groups, find some people to have a chat with and say, "Hey, when are you slow?" People love to talk about what they do, as I'm sure you do. Start that conversation up and find out when the dips are.

There are obvious slow seasons for some fields and some of those seasons happen like clockwork. For example, retail is always busy right before Christmas and usually has a slowdown in the middle of summer unless you have a store in a resort or vacation area. Likewise, restaurants are busy for a good portion of the year. Depending on where you are but you can usually bet that from January 1st until St Patrick's Day, you will be slower. That's the slowest season for most restaurants because people are paying off their credit cards from the holidays and have maybe made some health, fitness, or financial goals at the new year and they're trying to be good.

For most businesses, these clockwork periods are going to repeat every year and those are extremely easy to plan for. There are some slow seasons that are weather related, as there are some areas that are prone to hurricanes or blizzards, and people tend to not travel to those destinations during those times of year. Even if it's completely sporadic, for example, it's going to rain, which means nobody will come into your store that day. Then you can plan for it as well. There are also sometimes slow periods around presidential elections when there is a fear that it will affect the economy which makes people less apt to spend money.

There are of course lots of ways to have unplanned slow seasons, like global pandemics, but for the most part, your slow seasons are going to happen repeatedly every year. And as I said earlier, when I would be in a slow season, even 16 years in when I knew the patterns and I understood exactly what was going on, I still panicked and had anxiety over it. Nobody's expecting you to get over that completely, just know that you are not alone.

Understand there are some things that you can do in that slow season, so it does not feel out of control. I am a big fan of reviewing the year ahead for slow seasons and building them into your annual or 12-week plan, even financially budgeting for them. When you have a dip in sales, it is not catching you by surprise and completely turning your life upside down. Again, easier said than done. If you are a tiny business owner, your revenue most likely will fluctuate and it's hard to plan for emergencies. I get that. But as you are starting out, think about how a little planning ahead could make it so that you're not panicking during the slow seasons.

What about what to do with yourself when you are slow?

The things you never have time for:

Start with the things that you put off constantly but really need to be done, especially to move your business forward. That often involves a lot of marketing tasks, such as website refreshes, re-branding, a new logo designed, or changing the signage.

Deep cleaning and organizing of your space:

If you work from a home office, if you have a store, if you work in an office with other people, it's a great time to clean stuff out. Get rid of those files that you have in a drawer that you haven't used in years. Throw out the dried-out markers and dust the bookshelves. Check your city for places to donate unused office supplies, in Austin we have a place called Austin Creative Reuse where you can both donate and shop for so many supplies. They are great resources to ethically pass on your unwanted materials and pick up new ones.

Planning the next 12 weeks:

Slow seasons are also a really good time to plan. If you have not updated a marketing plan or investigated what your systems are, the slow time is the perfect time to do that. Regarding systems, the slow times are an excellent time to start looking at the things that you do repeatedly. You can start to create checklists and systems for these tasks, and you can make them more streamlined for when you are busy. I want to make something clear though. I don't want you to sit down and say, I'm going to now figure out what all my systems are, and it will be magical.

You really should implement systems while you're doing the work. It shouldn't be like, "oh, I have things that I do, I'm going to create systems for them." It should be, "oh it's kind of slow right now. While I'm packing these orders, let me write down the steps that I go through to get these orders out the door, all the way from getting them off of my website to dropping them at the post office. "You shouldn't just be making up what the system is. You should be taking advantage of the slow time and just putting into words what the steps are that you're doing.

Designing upcoming revenue streams and collections:

Slow times are also great for planning out the next few seasons. And that could look like thinking about how many customers you'd like to have and what you will do to get them. If you design or create your products and services, what will those collections of products or services look like? If you're not already, start to think about designing for seasonal releases, aka collections. As you grow in your business, the slow time can give you a nice block of time to create those upcoming collections. Perhaps you need a little bit of time to get samples and look at them months before the release.

Have you ever noticed that retail trade shows happen during January, early February, a little bit of March and then again in August? This is because those are the natural slow times for those industries. So, not only are the trade shows before the season that you are about to sell for, but the store owners and retailers can get away from things and go and look and shop and all of that. If you are in retail, trade shows, either for shopping or selling are a great, although expensive, slow-time filler.

Working with a service provider on your business:

If you want to work with a B2B service provider, like a designer, coach or consultant, or to work with somebody to do your advertising campaign or your social media or anything like that, the slow times are a great time to start working with them. There will usually be a good deal of work for you to do when you begin working together, so a slow time provides the perfect time to take on that commitment.

Batching content for future use:

This also could be a really good time to batch your content and social media to schedule out. What you should be doing is scheduling it a month or a quarter ahead of time and the slow times are the perfect time to schedule out months in advance if you can. If you are a maker and you know you have a show season coming up, start scheduling those social media posts, and you hopefully have your product ready to help you do this. Now think about what the things are that you wish you gave more attention to during the busy seasons? Perhaps it's something like writing blog posts ahead of time. Perhaps it's something like really looking at your client lists, your potential leads, or prospecting and starting to put together the contact information for people that you want to contact.

Keep this in mind as if it's slow in the industry you are reaching out to, you may be better off reaching out when it's busier. A lot of people that have been in industries for a while know that they're going to be slow, so they plan for it. That's when they take their annual vacation or when they just take a week off from work to catch up on stuff that they never get a chance to do like attend conferences and workshops that seem interesting.

Often when it's slow in their industry, if you're trying to

reach out to people, they don't want to work. They're taking a little bit of a mental break themselves. They're out of the office. In the weeks leading up to Christmas, understand that people may not be booking as many meetings and are starting to step back from work. Unless they are in sales, and then they are still going like gangbusters the last three weeks of the year. Pay attention to the patterns and begin to understand the industries you work in.

During your slow seasons, it's always smart to get in some of that relaxation. It will do you so well in the long-term and as I alluded to with the other people who are going through the slow time, a great time to step away. It's healthy for you to take time off and it's much easier to take time off when there's not much going on.

If you go on vacation when nobody is emailing you or calling you or trying to schedule things or ordering things, guess what? You won't feel like the world is ending when you go away. If there's nothing else you take away from this chapter, remember that vacations during the slow time are the best time to go because it's not stressful for you to be away from the business. Nobody will miss you being gone because they are not paying attention either.

The other thing to think about is to start to keep a list somewhere on your computer, in a notebook, or on a piece of paper on your desk, during the busy seasons. This will be a running list with the things that you want to get to but need more time for. The projects, new revenue streams, planning, trips, anything goes. Anything that you want to spend some time on, and you're frustrated that you're not getting to it. Then when you're slow, be it for a rainy day when nothing is happening or a week of vacations when a holiday falls midweek and everybody checks out, have some things on that list that you're excited about.

Be careful not to overestimate how much time you have when it's slow. Even a few weeks is not much time if you are working with a big branding company to help you rebrand, as that process alone can take months. If you are thinking that you're going to get all these things done, be realistic about the size of the project that you're trying to take on, but also keep that list so you can choose from the projects and say, which one do I want to take on financially and mentally right now? What do I have the capacity to do time-wise? When you are considering what to work on, ask yourself, can I afford to do this thing? Maybe not right now. Maybe you don't want to invest in that at this moment. Or you have saved up, let's do this. It's go time.

You'll soon learn the cycles. You'll be able to plan for them and budget for them, so you're not completely freaking out. If you're really stressed out, call up a friend or put a Facebook message in a group that you're in of people that are in your industry. If you network, bring it up because sometimes talking it out and knowing you're not alone is helpful. So have a conversation and open up about it.

And lastly, don't panic. It's hard when you are just starting out to have business stop, but sometimes it's stopping for everyone and it's just a slow season. It probably will be over before you know it. Don't freak out. It is maybe a time to think that if you really have a good amount of time during the slow season, for example, if you live in let's say a destination town where people are coming during June through September months and then the rest of the year is the off-season and slow. Think about having a different thing that you could be doing during those months. A freelance thing or a work thing or something that occupies your mind maybe gives you more income if you need it, but more to keep you engaged during that time.

I know a lot of fine artists who don't go out and do shows and don't sell online. Everything that they do is production for the holiday season when they sell at a big show where they bring in enough of an income to last them the year. It all depends on the cycles for your industry, how crazy busy you get in the busy seasons, how long your slow season is, but really that slow season should be used to do the work that you can't get to, to take a vacation, to enjoy yourself. To have some downtime to reflect, to think about what you want to do next. It's a time really that can benefit you greatly in business because if you are just go, go, go all the time, that would get exhausting, and you would burn out quickly. Enjoy that slow season.

Sum It Up:

- We all have slow seasons. It's great to figure out when yours will occur so you don't panic and use the time well.
- Keep a list of the tasks and projects you want to get done during the slower times of year. They are a great time to do the bigger projects we can't squeeze in when we're busy.
- Slow seasons are also a great time to take time off as you are in less demand. Enjoy the downtime!

Chapter 16:

Let's Do This!

Did you know that there are scientific ways to get yourself off the couch and into action? Or even better, there are systems you can have in place to keep you going when motivation is low. Let's talk about how you can not only motivate yourself to begin but how to set yourself up so even when you can't imagine continuing, you'll find the way to keep going.

What is it that keeps us from ticking off those to-do's and getting things done? It's our emotions. As humans, we can't ignore that we have feelings and that the key to motivating ourselves is to engage our emotions. So how do we do this? There are four ways for you to engage your emotions and motivate yourself.

The first is to get positive because dozens of books published in the last decade have taught us that happiness increases productivity and makes you more successful. We tend to procrastinate the most when we're in a bad mood. Who wants to do anything when you're in a bad mood? You get nothing done when you're in a bad mood, at least I don't. Maybe some of you do, but I do find that the better the mood I'm in, the more that I want to accomplish. Optimism is key.

The second is to monitor the progress you're making and celebrate it. Get excited about things. This is such a big part of motivation. When you feel confident about doing something, you're motivated and sure that you can accomplish what you're trying to do. You're excited about it. You can't wait to do it. And the main thing that makes us excited to do something is if we think we can do it. This is why it's so important both to do things and then to celebrate when you have done these things. Even if you have a tiny, tiny win, do a little dance in your office, pat yourself on the back, brag about it to a loved one who is excited about you doing things as much as you are.

What if we're not even to the point where we're having something to celebrate? What if we're still trying to get to the first step? How do you get positive then? How do you put yourself in a positive mindset? The easiest way that any of us can do that is to move our bodies. You want to literally get yourself into action. Take a little stroll around the neighborhood. Do some jumping jacks. Have a mini dance party.

Many studies prove that walking and exercise, and I'm not talking about doing CrossFit or anything extreme, I'm talking about simply elevating your heart rate a little, will greatly improve your mood. When you are needing that first step, go walk around the block or walk around your house. Just move a little bit.

For some people, talking to somebody who is positive really helps too. If you are in a group of friends that motivate each other, call one up, text one, tell them you need a little boost, or some motivation. They'll know what to do, they'll help you and they'll get you going. It's about getting yourself in that happy frame of mind. Getting into that positive mindset. It's making a mindset shift.

The third is to reward yourself because rewards are responsible for three-quarters of why we do things. Treat yourself whenever you accomplish something on your to-do list. And I don't mean like when you make the vet appointment for your dog, that's a little much. But if you are accomplishing something that is getting you closer to reaching your goals, reward yourself.

If you can't figure out a reward, you can try something called a commitment device. Give your friend $50. If you don't get the task done by 5:00 PM, you don't get your $50 back. If you do get it done, you get your $50 back. How's that for some motivation? But there are ways that you can treat yourself that you don't have to spend money and that you don't have to indulge.

You can give yourself time rewards. That's an effective way for those of us that try to cram everything into our schedule. We sometimes don't think that we're allowed to indulge our time doing certain things. Try something like, if you finish what you need to do, then on Saturday you can have four hours to take your dog on that hike that you love going on and you never think that you have enough time to do.

The fourth thing is peer pressure. Research shows that peer pressure helps kids more than it hurts them. Surround yourself with people you want to be like, it will become far less taxing to do what you should be doing. If you have people around you who are motivated and who are getting out there and doing great things and who you admire for their work ethic and for what they're accomplishing, you should be spending more time with those people and less time with the people that are not getting off the couch. It will really shift you in that direction to just be around people who are positive and are rewarding themselves and are doing things.

The best way to do this is to join groups. You can do anything from joining a Facebook group to groups in person. There are a lot of groups which for lack of a better term, often call themselves networking groups. More often though, they are about bringing together the people who are trying to accomplish things with their lives and who like to be around similarly motivated people. Being in a group like that can go a long way to keep you feeling motivated.

You can pull together a group of friends or create your own mastermind group. You'll want to have people in that group that you can reach out to and get in touch with when you're needing to have a little bit of a reminder of what path you're on, especially if you're sharing with them what you want to be accomplishing. When you're coming to them and saying that you're not feeling it, they will know what the bigger picture is and can help you get back on track.

That's why Masterminds do well, because you understand each other's motivators, the end results that you're each striving for. The people in your group have heard you open up and be vulnerable, so they probably understand why you are all of a sudden exhibiting a lack of motivation. They might remind you that you're just experiencing this fear that you've had in the past. They'll encourage you to push through this. This is nothing. This is just your regular habit or your regular pattern that you fall back on. You need to get through this.

What if none of those things that I just talked about work? Well, having systems in place makes achieving your goals as easy as possible, even when motivation is low. Because motivation comes in waves. The most excitement you'll have is for the first few months of starting a business or a project. Motivation will be just flowing out of your fingertips like rainbows and sunshine. And then sometimes, there's just no motivation when we need it. The well feels dry. We push things off to tomorrow. We decide that our future self can deal with it. But our future self is lazy.

What are you supposed to do then, if you're sitting here thinking, all right, I'm not going to be able to motivate myself? Nobody else will be able to motivate me. So how am I going to get things done? The first step is that you're going to plan for failure. You're going to get comfortable with trying more things. You're going to be willing to fail.

That's the most important part of this. The people that have success stories typically can list off the 300 ways that they failed before they succeeded. The pitches that they made for their book, dozens of times, money that they tried to get, hundreds of times. Fail, fail, fail, fail, and then they keep going.

In planning for success, you should plan to fail because if you're not willing to fail, you will not succeed. The difference between average and top performers is that average people give up when they fail. Top performers keep pushing until they succeed.

Make a list of everything you need to do to reach your goal and then set up systems to make it impossible to fail. What do I mean by systems? Let's look at exercise and health goals because almost everybody can relate to these. With exercise, it is said that if you exercise in the morning it is the better time to do it if you are prone to procrastinate on exercise or if you are trying to lose weight or accomplish a goal. If you exercise in the afternoon, you will go harder and you will enjoy it more.

I personally have always been an afternoon exerciser. It came from playing sports in school and I have stayed in that pattern. However, that morning exercise so I can't put it off, is looking a lot more attractive as my schedule gets more and more chaotic. If I wait to exercise at the end of the day, I'm often exhausted or a meeting replaces it. And then it just ends up not getting done over and over. It's easy to see why one of the best systems to get yourself exercising is to do it first thing in the morning. Even to include laying out your gym clothes the night before so that you wake up, and there are your gym clothes. You put the clothes on, and you exercise. You're basically not giving your brain a chance to say no but putting yourself on autopilot.

Another example is if you have the desire to switch from coffee to tea, you can create a system where you remove all the coffee things from the kitchen. You replace them with all the tea things. Maybe you have an electric kettle, maybe you have the teabags in a cute little container on the counter and then have the mug ready. When you get up in the morning, there is no coffee to make, you just go right to the tea things instead of the coffee things. You're making it extra simple to make the tea and to accomplish that goal.

Do you want to read more books? Make it easy to read.

Always have books around you. Have them in spots around your house where you'll see them, and you'll pick them up when you have a few minutes. Carry one with you when you go out. When I decided that I wanted to pursue a goal of reading more books, I started doing this. I had a stack of books set up by a comfy chair in the bedroom. I've always had them by the bed anyway, but I started going to bed earlier to give myself more time to read. Then I started putting them all over the dining room table. I have a large table in my office and now that has books on it. There are books everywhere, so if I have 10 minutes and I have kicked myself off the Internet when I was doing nothing, I will read. This made it so that I am now reading three times the number of books that I had been reading when I first set that goal, so look at that. Having them around really did work.

The next part of the setting up systems is to put it on your schedule or in your calendar. Fancy tools don't matter as much as we think. All you need is a pen, a scrap of paper, or your notes app to achieve your goals. Execution is more important than the tactic itself, meaning that getting the thing done is more important than how you get it done. We tend to spend a lot of time setting up our to-do lists in our calendars, and our systems and all of that. I am a big fan of being totally into your calendar and your system planning. However, don't end up spending so much time planning that you haven't left yourself the time to do the thing.

Monica Geller had a great moment with this in the early seasons of Friends[49] when she booked a catering job. She planned, and she planned, and she planned, but she didn't leave enough time to do the things. Chaos ensued. Remember that you want to avoid spending all your time planning or you won't have time to do the thing. You don't have infinite time. Time is finite, be aware of wasted time. When you're planning out your week, include a block of time for your actual planning and keep it to that.

I'm a big fan of using an online to-do app[50] to be able to set recurring alerts so I don't have to remember to put things in my planner that come up every single week or even every single day. They just pop up automatically. But don't spend all your time looking for the perfect one, find something, put it into place, use it. If you don't like it, a few months later you can switch, but it's really about execution. That is the most important part.

The third part of creating these systems is to develop laser focus. Yes, emergencies come up. We had a situation in our family last week. I was not directly involved with it, but dealing with it emotionally and having conversations about things took up a lot of my time and more importantly, it ended up taking up a lot of my mental space, so I had a hard time focusing.

49 Season 2, Episode 11: The One with the Lesbian Wedding

50 I'm obsessed with Todoist: https://todoist.com/

That happens. Emergencies are going to come up. Your child or your parent or a close relative or friend is going to end up in the hospital at some point. You may end up in the hospital at some point. Don't feel like you must give up on your goals when emergencies strike, you are simply pausing them and changing your focus until the emergency passes. Emergencies come up; you will get past them.

Besides losing focus when dealing with emergencies, many of us will sabotage one goal by shifting focus to another. This is one of my own downfalls. I want to have 19 big goals going on at a time. I want to be working on all the things at once. But you can't work on all the things because if you do try to work on multiple goals at once, nothing really gets done. You don't make progress on anything, so you want to focus on one to three big goals at a time.

Work on these three goals and get it so you are no longer having to take all your focus to set your new habits and get systems in place for these big goals. When the work to accomplish these becomes part of your routine (about 60 days to set a habit) you can start to work on different goals. You have a long life, working on only three goals at a time will yield huge results.

Write your goals down by hand. Write down what is motivating you to do that goal. Why are you wanting to accomplish your goal? It is amazing that as soon as you write things down, your brain wants to solve that problem, so write down the things that you want to do, and your brain will start working on it. Your brain will start laser focusing on it. If you put laser focus on your goals, your brain will think it's happening and you will get your goals done. And then, I know I said three things, but once you are putting all your systems in place, test and adjust them, there's always room for improvement.

But you need to get working on them before you start testing and adjusting. Because as we talked about at the beginning, action is the most important part. As we talked about in all of these, really doing the thing is the most important part.

Sum It Up:

- The first few months of a new business are the easiest time to stay motivated, but then what? Understanding the ways to get yourself motivated and keep yourself going can be a huge help when you're feeling frustrated in the beginning.
- Create systems to help yourself work instead of doing things which work against you. Make it easy to get things done.
- Don't fall into the trap of spending all of your time planning and never giving yourself time to do the actual work.
- Keep going!!!

Acknowledgements

Thank you to my person, Adam Fujawa, for cheering me on and dealing with waking the dogs up at 5am to write.

Thank you to my editor, Mallory Lehenbauer, who taught me everything about writing books and caught so many typos. So many typos.

Thank you to my cover designer Joanna Holden for bringing the book to beautiful life.

Thank you to Angie Brinkley, Corinne Arles and Jocelyn Lovelle for listening as I talked through it, holding me accountable and supporting me through the writing and editing process.

A HUGE thank you to all of the talented, tiny business owners out there who I wrote this for, especially those who are my clients, in my circle, and are Doers. You are all doing great and inspire me every day!!

Bibliography

Achor, S. (2011). *The Happiness Advantage.* Random House.

Allen, D. (2015). *Getting Things Done.* Penguin Publishing Group.

Band, Z. (2019). *Success Is in Your Sphere: Leverage the Power of Relationships to Achieve Your Business Goals.* The McGraw-Hill Companies.

Beckwith, H. (2012). *Selling the invisible.* New York: Grand Central Publishing.

Blake, J. (2017). *Pivot: The only move that matters is your next one.* New York: Portfolio/Penguin.

Broughton, P. D. (2013). *The art of the sale: Learning from the masters about the business of life.* New York: Penguin Books.

Brown, B. (2015). *Daring greatly: How the courage to be vulnerable transforms the way we live, love, parent, and lead.* NY, NY: Avery, an imprint of Penguin Random House.

Buelow, B. L. (2015). *The introvert entrepreneur: Amplify your strengths and create success on your own terms.* NY, NY: Perigee, an imprint of Penguin Random House LLC.

Cialdini, R. B., & Garde, N. (1987). *Influence.* Paris: A. Michel.

Clark, D. (2017). *Reinventing you define your brand, imagine your future.* Boston, MA: Harvard Business Review Press.

Cloutier, G., & Marshall, S. (2010). *Profits aren't everything, they're the only thing: No-nonsense rules from the ultimate contrarian and small business guru*. New York: Harper Business.

Collins, J. C. (2009). *Good to great: Why some companies make the leap ... and others don't.* New York, NY: Collins.

Covey, Stephen R./ Merrill, A. Roger/ Merrill, Rebecca R. (2017). *First Things First.* Simon & Schuster.

Diliberto, G. (2016). *Diane von Furstenberg: A life unwrapped.* New York, NY: Dey St.

Ducker, C. (2018). *Rise of the youpreneur: The definitive guide to becoming the go-to leader in your industry and building a future-proof business.* Cambridge, UK: 4C Press.

Duckworth, A. (2016). *Grit.* Simon & Schuster.

Duhigg, C. (2014). *The power of habit: Why we do what we do in life and business*. New York: Random House Trade Paperbacks.

Duhigg, C. (2017). *Smarter, faster, better: The secrets of being productive.* London: Random House.

Dweck, C. S. (2017). *Mindset: Changing the way you think to fulfil your potential.* New York: Robinson.

Ecko̅, M. (2015). *Unlabel: Selling you without selling out.* New York: Touchstone Books.

Ferrazzi, K. R. (2014). *Never Eat Alone: And Other Secrets to Success, One Relationship at a Time*. Random House.

Ferriss, T. (2008). *The 4-hour workweek: Escape 9-5, live anywhere, and join the new rich*. London: Vermilion.

Ferriss, T. (2017). *Tools of titans: The tactics, routines, and habits of billionaires, icons, and world-class performers*. Boston: Houghton Mifflin Harcourt.

Ferriss, T. (2018). *Tribe of Mentors: Short Life Advice from the Best in the World.* Boston: Houghton Mifflin Harcourt Publishing Company.

Flynn, P. (2016). *Will it fly?: How to test your next business idea so you don't waste your time and money.* San Diego, CA: SPI Publications.

Flynn, P. (2019). *Superfans: The easy way to stand out, grow your tribe, and build a successful business.* San Diego: Get Smart Books.

Fried, J., Hansson, D. H., & Popescu, C. (2011). *Rework.* Bucureşti: Publica.

Gerber, M. E. (2017). *The E-myth revisited: Why most small businesses don't work and what to do about it.* New York: Harper Collins.

Gladwell, M. (2015). *David and Goliath.* Penguin.

Gladwell, M. (2019). *Outliers: The story of success.* New York: Back Bay Books, Little, Brown and Company.

Glei, J. K. (n.d.). *Manage your day-to-day.* Las Vegas, NV: Amazon Publ.

Godin, S. (2007). *Permission marketing.* London: Pocket.

Godin, S., & Horst, M. T. (2010). *Purple cow.* Utrecht: Lev.

Godin, S. (2014). *Tribes we need you to lead us.*

Godin, S. (2018). *Linchpin: Are you indispensable?* London: Piatkus.

Godin, S. (2020). *The Practice.* UK: Penguin Business.

Goldman, J., & Zagat, A. (2016). *Getting to like: How to boost your personal and professional brand to expand opportunities, grow your business, and achieve financial success.* Wayne, NJ: Career Press.

Grant, A. M. (2013). *Give and take: The revolutionary worldview that drives success.* London: Weidenfeld & Nicolson.

Hall, E. (1973). *Why we do what we do: A look at psychology.* Boston: Houghton Mifflin.

Hardy, D. (2012). *The Compound Effect.* Carroll & Graf; Csm editor.

Harris, R. (2011). *The confidence gap: From fear to freedom*. London: Robinson.

Hoffman, J., & Finkel, D. (2016). *Scale: Seven proven principles to grow your business and get your life back*. Troy, MI: Business News Publishing.

Holiday, R. (2014). *Growth hacker marketing*. Place of publication not identified: Profile Books.

Holiday, R. (2014). *The obstacle is the way: The timeless art of turning trials into triumph*. New York: Portfolio/Penguin.

Holmes, C. (2007). *The ultimate sales machine: Turbocharge your business with relentless focus on 12 key strategies*. New York: Portfolio.

Hyatt, M. (2019). *Your best year ever*. Embassy Books.

Hyatt, M. (2019). *Free to focus: A total productivity system to achieve more by doing less*. Grand Rapids, MI: Baker Book, a division of Baker Publishing Group.

Jarvis, P. (2020). *Company of one: Why staying small is the next big thing for business*. Boston, MA: Mariner Books, Houghton Mifflin Harcourt.

Jiwa, B. (2018). *Story driven: You don't need to compete when you know who you are*. Australia: Perceptive Press.

Kaufman, J. (2012). *The personal MBA: A world-class business education in a single volume*. London: Portfolio.

Kawasaki, G. (2012). *Enchantment: The art of changing hearts, minds and actions*. London: Portfolio Penguin.

Keenan. (2018). *Gap selling: Getting the customer to yes: How problem-centric selling increases sales by changing everything you know about relationships, overcoming objections, closing and price*. Sales Guy Publishing.

Keller, G. (2014). *One thing*. John Murray Lt.

King, S. (2000). *On writing: A memoir*. London: Hodder & Stoughton.

Knight, P. (2018). *Shoe Dog*. Simon & Schuster.

Koch, R. (2017). *80/20 principle*. Nicholas Brealey Pub.

Krawcheck, S. (2017). *Own it: The power of women at work*. New York: Crown.

Levesque, R. (2019). *Ask.: The counterintuitive online method to discover exactly what your customers want to buy ... create a mass of raving fans ... and take any business to the next level.* Carlsbad, CA: Hay House.

Mackey, J., & Sisodia, R. (2014). *Conscious capitalism: Liberating the heroic spirit of business*. Boston, MA: Harvard Business Review Press.

Macy, B. (2014). *Factory Man*. Little Brown & Company.

McCormack, W. J., & McCormack, M. H. (1984). *What they don't teach you at Harvard Business School.* London: Harper Collins.

McNally, D. (2006). *Be your own brand: a breakthrough formula for standing out from the crowd.* San Francisco, CA: Berrett-Koehler.

Michalowicz, M. (2016). *Profit first: A simple system to transform any business from a cash-eating monster to a money-making machine*. Opladen: Budrich Inspirited.

Morin, A. (2015). *13 things mentally strong people don't do*. London: Thorsons.

Newport, C. (2018). *Deep work: Rules for focused success in a distracted world.* Place of publication not identified: Grand Central Pub.

Pang, A. S., & Huffington, A. S. (2018). *Rest: Why you get more done when you work less*. UK: Penguin Life.

Patel, N., Vlaskovits, P., & Koffler, J. (2016). *Hustle: The power to charge your life with money, meaning, and momentum*. London: Vermilion.

Pink, D. H. (2009). *Drive: The surprise truth about what motivates us*. New York: Riverhead Books.

Pofeldt, E. (2021). *The million-dollar, one-person business: Make great money, work the way you like, have the life you want.* California: Lorena Jones Books.

Pressfield, S. (2015). *Do the work.* Black Irish Entertainment.

Ries, A., & Trout, J. (1994). *The 22 immutable laws of marketing: Violate them at your own risk.* New York, NY: HarperBusiness.

Rubin, G. (2016). *Better Than Before.* Hodder.

Rubin, G. (2018). *Happiness Project.* New York: HarperCollins.

Schwartz, D. J. (2009). *Magic of thinking big.* Mumbai: R.R. Sheth.

Sivers, D. (2015). *Anything you want: 40 lessons for a new kind of entrepreneur.* London: Portfolio Penguin.

Stanier, M. B. (2010). *Do more great work: Stop the busywork, and start the work that matters.* New York: Workman Pub.

Tharp, T., & Reiter, M. (2006). *The creative habit: Learn it and use it for life: A practical guide.* New York: Simon & Schuster.

Thiel, P., & Masters, B. (2015). *Zero to one notes on startups, or how to build the future.* London: Virgin Books.

Underhill, P. (2009). *Why We Buy: The Science of Shopping - Updated and Revised for the Internet, the Global Consumer and Beyond.* New York, NY: Simon & Schuster.

Voss, C. (2017). *Never Split the Difference.* England: Cornerstone.

Weiss, A. (2014). *Million dollar launch: How to kick-start a successful consulting practice in 90 days.* New York: McGraw-Hill.

Wu, T. (2018). *The curse of bigness: Antitrust in the new Gilded Age.* New York: Columbia Global Reports.

About the Author

Sierra Bailey is a business educator and talented, tiny business owner expert. In the decades of running her own successful tiny businesses, sitting on boards, being a business educator who helps other tiny businesses thrive, and creating a popular Facebook community, Sierra has learned one huge thing: Running a tiny business and doing the thing you love (and are super talented at) isn't about living up to the myth that more employees is better. It's about creating YOUR business YOUR way.

She lives in Austin with her husband Adam and their two rat-terrier rescues, Fiona and Bessie. When not helping tiny business owners, Sierra can be found with her nose in a book and a cup of coffee in her hand. Find out more at mssierrabailey.com

www.ingramcontent.com/pod-product-compliance
Lightning Source LLC
Chambersburg PA
CBHW030504210326
41597CB00013B/781

* 9 7 8 1 7 3 7 4 7 8 8 1 2 *